The Contributors

Christina Barlow is a highly experienced riding instructor based in South Africa, where she runs and teaches at her own equestrian training centre. She has spent many years working with nervous riders.

Julie Goodnight has been a full-time equine professional for more that 20 years, with experience ranging from dressage and jumping to reining and wilderness riding. Julie owns and runs Goodnight Training Stables, Colorado, and conducts horsemanship clinics for riders and horses of all ability levels, including fear management courses. She is a frequent speaker at clinics, conferences and horse fairs all over the USA, and has produced several instructional videos.

Abigail Hogg has spent a lifetime working with often very troubled horses. As assistant to Lucy Rees, author of *The Horse's Mind*, a seminal work on equine psychology, she travelled through Spain offering both horses and their owners a more understanding approach to training. Abigail is a member of the Equine Behaviour Forum and the author of *The Horse Behaviour Handbook*. Her insight into horse behaviour provides an opportunity for fear-free learning for both horse and owner.

Liz Morrison LLB, BHSI(SM) is a licensed NLP Master Practitioner and international level 2 riding instructor. Over the past five years her courses about applying NLP to riding have been attended by hundreds of riders, instructors and examiners. When not training with teams and individuals around the world, Liz competes in affiliated dressage and show jumping on her own horses. She is the author of *Simple Steps to Riding Success*.

Sharon Shinwell DIP Couns DIP HP (NC) NRHP, has competed, bred and owned horses for over 25 years. She is a qualified hypno-psychotherapist and counsellor and has combined her knowledge of the human psyche, especially that of the rider, with her knowledge and experience of hypnotherapy, to produce a successful range of self-hypnosis CDs known as the *Confident Rider Series*.

CONTRIBUTORS

Christina Barlow

Julie Goodnight

Abigail Hogg

Liz Morrison

Sharon Shinwell

Ride with Confidence!

Practical and inspirational advice
to help you deal with your fear and
enjoy your riding

FOREWORD BY KELLY MARKS

David & Charles

A DAVID & CHARLES BOOK

David & Charles is a subsidiary of F+W (UK) Ltd.,
an F+W Publications Inc. company

First published in 2004

Distributed in North America
by F+W Publications, Inc.
4700 East Galbraith Road
Cincinnati, OH 45236
1-800-289-0963

A catalogue record for this book is available from the British Library.

ISBN 0 7153 1809 8 paperback
ISBN 0 7153 1822 5 hardback

Printed in Singapore by KHL
for David & Charles
Brunel House   Newton Abbot   Devon

Commissioning Editor Jane Trollope
Desk Editor Sarah Martin
Art Editor Sue Cleave
Project Editor Sue Grout
Production Controller Jennifer Campbell

Visit our website at www.davidandcharles.co.uk

David & Charles books are available from all good bookshops; alternatively you
can contact our Orderline on (0)1626 334555 or write to us at FREEPOST
EX2110, David & Charles Direct, Newton Abbot, TQ12 4ZZ (no stamp required
UK mainland).

Contents

When nerves were 'invented'...

KELLY MARKS
Intelligent Horsemanship

If sex was invented in 1963 (according to the poet Philip Larkin*) then I think it's fair to say that fear for the horse rider or 'nerves' wasn't really invented until some time in the 1990s. Certainly I cannot recall any of the jump jockeys I raced against during my career ever mentioning the 'f' word. In the bravado world of racing the very idea of it was unthinkable. Nowadays, thank goodness, fear is allowed. People don't have to pretend, even to themselves (unless of course they choose to) that they are not frightened of these large, often unpredictable, creatures.

Never before this book, though, have I seen so much good information in one place about this last taboo of horsemanship: 'fear'. Whether people will feel they have to carry it home from the bookshop wrapped in brown paper, or say they are just buying it 'for a friend' remains to be seen. I seriously hope that as many instructors buy this book as riders who are out to conquer their fears. It could really help so many people, and a part of me feels that rescuing dreams is not so far removed from rescuing lives.

A friend of mine went to a hypnotherapist and was successfully treated for her phobia of spiders. Her mother decided to go to the same therapist to overcome her fear of flying. 'I'm sorry I really can't help you' the therapist replied 'because *that's* a perfectly valid fear!' It's unfortunate, perhaps, to come across a therapist who is just as doubtful about the wisdom of flying as you are, but it isn't essential for this lady to take plane trips and she has settled quite happily for summer holidays in Scotland and taking the Channel Tunnel to Europe. In the same way I don't think anyone can say they have to ride horses, it's a choice we can make after we have carefully measured the pros and cons. The fact is it certainly can be a dangerous hobby and it would be irresponsible to encourage a nervous person to ride by simply saying 'Take Rescue Remedy™

* Annus Mirabilis, *High Windows*, Philip Larkin (Faber & Faber, 1974)

and keeping saying these affirmations: "I am a very confident rider, I am a very confident rider", I'm sure you'll be fine...'

There can be a number of reasons why you are nervous about riding. It could be due to an accident you've had or seen someone else have (actually this can be worse – when you fall off yourself it often happens so quickly you don't really know what happened!). It could be due to a new horse you are unsure of, or new circumstances. A change of lifestyle is a well known factor in bringing about more 'caution' in professional jump jockeys, hence the expression 'he went at a married man's canter'. The awareness of having something (or someone) to lose may be the first time the rider has ever even considered the consequences of falling. Your fear could even seemingly come from nowhere and appear completely 'irrational'.

If you are nervous at all in any circumstances, first of all I would like to say a big 'well done' for admitting it in the first place. There are not hundreds of nervous riders in Britain but thousands. If you admit to the fact and take responsibility for it then you can start to do something positive to conquer your fears in the safest and fairest way to you and the horses you are involved with. Much better than blaming your horse for being 'nervy' and prone to napping (because he very likely will be) and punishing him for being 'ungenuine' and refusing jumps, it is the way forward to a more considered, contemplative and possibly intelligent way of riding and interacting around horses.

I run an organization called Intelligent Horsemanship (some of you may have heard of it!), which is dedicated to bringing the best horsemanship ideas together, and to promoting the understanding and fair treatment of equines. We run clinics and courses on horsemanship and sometimes we have students who are quite nervous about handling horses generally. Our aim by the time they leave is for them to be far more self-assured when dealing with strange horses, but not, I hasten to add, through 'gung-ho' bravery or by psyching themselves up, but because they have learned to some extent to be careful and cautious, and to approach horses in such a manner that they are putting themselves at the minimum risk of being hurt. It's generally the people who come into horses later in life who put themselves in the most danger. I don't know whether this is because being round ponies and horses when you are very young creates some intuitive sense of preservation around horses, or whether it's just a fact that the good old Pony Club drilled those little, yet so important, points into your head

– check your girths, turn your horse's head towards you at the gate before letting him go, don't pat strange horses on the bottom! Either way, a better understanding of horses will make you safer.

A major part of our work on the courses or with owners of so-called 'horses with problems' as well as general 'horse sense' is to teach people 'body awareness' around horses. I think this book will help people, instructors and students alike, to add to this an emotional awareness, where they can truly look at how they are feeling and examine the validity of that feeling, and decide on the best course of action to take.

Although I know of cases where affirmations, hypnotherapy and NLP techniques have been invaluable to people (with Pippa Funnell, the top eventer, being one of the first professional riders to 'come out' about how this has helped her) it's also of vital importance, as this book appreciates, to begin with an analysis of how valid your fears really are. How safe are your riding experiences? What is it exactly that you fear the most? And what is the likelihood that it could happen? Although there are accidents that come totally out of the blue, calculating the risk factor of each situation shouldn't be too difficult. For example: an experienced rider with a good seat walking a quiet, aged horse round an indoor school might have a risk factor of one per cent. A very inexperienced, unstable rider jumping a novice, unschooled, highly strung horse round a cross-country course on a wet and windy day would be nearer 99 per cent. Which brings us to one of my favourite questions: 'What's the difference between intelligent people and stupid people?' 'Well... intelligent people do intelligent things and stupid people do stupid things!'

The next time you are going out to ride and are feeling fear (as opposed to being genuinely excited by a competition, an entirely different thing) do a risk analysis of the situation. Let's say you are nervous of taking your horse on a three mile ride alone, on a route around where he is kept. Don't feel bad because you 'shouldn't be' feeling nervous – maybe you should. What is it exactly you feel might happen? Is he prone to over-excitement when he's out in open spaces? If he did have a buck and a kick, would you be able to stay on? Are you worried about falling off and no one knowing where you are? I suggest you get out a pen and paper and make a list of your concerns. Once you get your worries in the open then you can get your mind working on practical solutions. Write down practical solutions to the worries on your list. Solutions may include: don't go on the ride for the time being, keep consistently having good quality lessons with an understanding instructor so that your seat and riding position are so strong your confidence soars. If you are more confident with your horse on the ground you may consider leading him round the route (it'll get you fitter as well!). Take sensible precautions to protect yourself: wear a back protector, use a neckstrap, take a mobile phone with you (but still always tell someone where you are going and what time you are expecting to be back). You may have to look realistically at your horse. Is he too big for you to handle? Would an older, less highly strung horse suit you better? Would he be perfectly all right if he perhaps had more time out in his field, or less high-energy feed, or perhaps he really needs a companion on this ride to start with?

Don't think that professionals and top riders never feel fear. They work very hard to prepare their horses, control the conditions they perform under, and put themselves and their horses at the least risk. If they were riding under some of the conditions that you occasionally see at a local show – for example, a totally unschooled horse with no mouth and an ill-fitting saddle entering a jumping competition – they'd probably be frightened!

Ultimately, to improve at anything we have to come out of our comfort zone. However, it's wise for both horse and rider to work their way up in realistically small steps. For instance, many people do have the odd fall jumping in the early days, particularly if they are working with a novice jumper. It makes more sense to admit that this can happen and start your schooling off in a manége with a nice soft surface than just pretending it could never happen.

Don't feel you have to 'go it alone' either, but bear in mind that an instructor who suits one student really well may not be right for another. Some students need to be asked at every step how they are feeling and whether they are ready to do more. I have also seen students make tremendous improvements under the old school 'Come on, you can do it!' approach. It's for us as teachers to assess what is the best approach for students and when we go and have lessons ourselves, to give feedback as to what helps us most.

Finally, don't EVER let anyone embarrass you for being nervous. Listen to your fears and make the risk analysis. It may be that your fear is just another word for common sense.

Kelly's top ten tips for handling fear

O Do a risk analysis and decide what it is sensible for you to do and exactly what it is you would like to do.

O Work very hard to minimize your risks by ensuring you have a very stable riding position and are using the right equipment, including a saddle that is comfortable to both you and your horse.

O Find a good instructor who you can talk frankly with. It is wise to approach the subject during your initial phone call and then remind the instructor when you see them for the lesson. Some instructors specialize in nervous riders and it may be worthwhile seeking them out.

O 'Under-horse' yourself. Ride a horse that is so quiet you find it boring and want to move on to one that is more exciting – this clearly means you are getting more confident! Alternatively you may find this horse is actually perfect for you, which makes him the ideal solution!

O If you feel that, in fact, the risks you are taking are extremely low and your fear by now is quite inappropriate – just act 'as if' you are confident. Simple as it may sound, this technique has been used successfully by thousands of people in thousands of different situations. Try it.

O Some people have found it helpful to take the responsible role, that is by constantly reassuring the horse and telling him not to be worried. Singing is another popular option and also reminds you to breathe! Yes, and while we're at it:

○ Don't forget to breathe! This is one of the reasons why singing is helpful, but it may also be helpful to practise deep diaphragmatic breathing off your horse while visualizing yourself riding.

○ Relaxation for the head and neck are useful as well. Gently turn the neck and shrug the shoulders, then ensure they are down and relaxed. Funny how our shoulders can end up so close to our ears when we are under stress!

○ Explore other alternative methods of fear control. Many people have found methods such as NLP, hypnotheraphy, visualization, affirmations or taking Bach Flower Remedies helpful (see page 188).

○ Share your concerns with like-minded people: for example, check out the Intelligent Horsemanship website Discussion Group (see page 188) and start or join a thread for nervous riders. This wonderful group inspired me to write about fear in the first place. It has long been known that discussing your concerns with supportive people can help a great deal, at the very least reassuring you that you are not alone.

1

Managing
Your Fear

Julie Goodnight

'Learning to manage a fear of horses is an attainable
goal for anyone, by following this systematic
process of intellectualizing the fear, developing
a plan for recovery, learning acting skills for
physical and mental control, and improving
horsemanship and safety skills.'

Identifying fear

Horses are much more adept at recognizing fear than we humans. Not only are horses much more attuned to the subtleties of body language and non-verbal communication, they are also much keener when it comes to picking up the emotions of other animals in their environment. Since horses are prey animals, reliant on the herd for their very own survival, they are programmed to monitor the emotions and actions of the animals in their herd and to act accordingly. Horses reflect the emotions of their herd mates, thus the emotion of fear can run rampant through the herd like wildfire.

There are many subtle signs which horses pick up which indicate fearfulness, whether in other horses or in humans. Tense muscles, quick jerky movements and shallow breathing are just a few of the indicators. Horses sense fear; they see it, hear it, smell it and feel it, and for their own protection, they will mirror the fear they sense around them.

This ability of horses to recognize and react to fearfulness compounds the issue of our fear of riding or handling them. Because horses are programmed to reflect the emotions of their herd mates and because they have no other way of thinking of us than as a member of the herd, it is important to learn to control our emotions and to present a picture of complete confidence to the horse. We often refer to this ability as 'fake it until you make it', and it is a fantastic skill to develop.

Physical symptoms

In learning to cope with a fear of horses, it is important to be able to recognize the symptoms of fear in your own body and mind so that you can control the emotion rather than have the emotion control you. Learning to monitor and control the physical manifestations of fear in your own body will not only help you feel more confident, but will also help the horses around you to stay calm and quiet. Individually or in combinations,

It is important to learn to control our emotions and to present a picture of complete confidence to the horse.

there are many physical symptoms associated with the emotion of fear, and chances are you've felt a few of them yourself.

Learning to recognize these symptoms early on as fear sets in can make the difference in your ability to control this emotion and keep it in check.

Facing up to fear

Fear is actually a useful emotion because it keeps us safe. Without it, we would plunge blindly into reckless and dangerous activities. There's certainly nothing wrong with being afraid of horses; they are large unpredictable animals, capable of spontaneous violent reactions. Everyone feels fear to some degree; you would have to be an idiot not to. But when fearfulness impacts your enjoyment of horses, it is time to do something about it.

Unfortunately, fear is seldom mentioned around horse people and there seems to be a stigma associated with it. Because I conduct clinics on coping with a fear of horses many people approach me about the issue. I know for a fact that a fear of horses is extremely common, even though it is rarely discussed. In dealing with this issue yourself, it is very important that you feel comfortable discussing it with your trainer, your riding companions or your partner. Hopefully, these people will be very supportive and understanding of your situation, and will be willing to help you with your plan for recovery.

Common symptoms associated with fear

- Breathlessness
- Heart fluttering, chest pain or pressure
- A sensation of drowning or suffocating
- Dizziness or vertigo
- A sense of detachment from reality
- Tingling sensations
- Heat or cold waves
- Sweating
- Dry mouth
- Fainting, trembling, shaking
- A fear of dying or becoming mad
- A fear of losing control

Understanding fear

There are two types of fear and most of us suffer from a little of both. Post-traumatic fear is the result of an accident or injury, while general anxiety is an emotion created in our own minds. It is important to thoroughly understand the two types and to know where your fear originates so that you can have an objective outlook, begin to intellectualize the fear and develop a plan to manage it.

Post-traumatic fear develops after an incident that caused a physical or emotional injury. It is easy to understand how a physical injury can lead to fearfulness, but sometimes we tend to disregard the emotional wounds that can result from the frightening experience of a 'near miss'.

Whether your injuries are physical or emotional, it is extremely important that you give yourself time to heal after a traumatic incident. Not only do your bones and flesh need to mend before exposure to physical strain, but you also need the time to replenish your emotional energy and heal your spirit.

I am not a big believer in the old axiom, 'Get right back on the horse that bucked you off.' Whereas in some instances this may serve a purpose, when we are dealing with real injuries, it is likely that more harm than good may be done. Furthermore, while in the midst of a frightening experience, it is more likely that your fears will be compounded rather than eliminated, and your tendency to make mistakes is strong.

case study

My own experience The experience I had that led me to this conclusion actually had nothing to do with horses, but was a situation where I 'got right back on'. I was kayaking in some rather challenging white water in a remote wilderness gorge in New Mexico when suddenly I found myself pinned between two rocks, with tons of water gushing by me every second. Since I was the last one through the rapid in my group, I watched helplessly and yelled at the top of my lungs for help as the rest of my cohorts paddled on through the gorge, focused on their own survival and paying no attention to what had become of me. The fear and panic began to boil over as

It is extremely important that you give
  yourself time to heal after a trauma.

I realized that I was helplessly stuck between two boulders, with water rushing around me up to my neck. Although I was unhurt and could still breath, all I could think about was what would happen if I couldn't get out or if my boat was pushed through just a few more centimetres, causing me to be sucked into the sieve that was created by the two rocks.

Eventually my friends noticed my absence and set off upstream with a rope to rescue me. Although it was a complicated process, I managed to get free and pull my boat out unharmed, at least physically. By then I was shaking all over with fear but I had no choice, being in a remote gorge with walls hundreds of meters high, but to paddle the remaining stretch of river, some three or four hours through even more challenging rapids.

At every turn of the river and at each new rapid, I became even more frightened, to the point of nausea, crying and shaking all over. It was an interminably miserable experience and totally exacerbated my fear. Although I stuck with the sport for some time after that, I never really regained my joy and passion for white water and eventually set it aside to focus on other sports. Although I was not physically hurt in this incident, the emotional injury was severe and with each successive rapid, that wound was torn open just a little bit more.

Fear memories

Research was conducted at Colorado State University on fear memories in cattle and horses. Although it was not intended to have implications for humans, as I read the study I was struck by how much the research actually related to post-traumatic fear in our species.

The thesis of the study was that when a horse or cow is injured, a 'fear memory' is logged in the amygdala, part of the lower brain where subconscious thought and instinctive behaviour is controlled. The research project showed that once a fear memory is logged, it will be in the animal's brain for the rest of its life. For instance, if the very first time a horse is loaded into a horse trailer he throws his head up and cuts his face, a fear memory is logged into his brain. For the rest of the horse's life, every time he walks up to the trailer, that fear memory will come to his consciousness. We can over-ride the fear memory with training, but we can never erase it entirely.

Thankfully, I have never been seriously hurt around horses, although I have certainly had my fair share of bumps, bruises and the occasional concussion. Years ago, when I was much younger and much dumber than I am now, I did a stupid thing that resulted in my getting injured. By the way, every time I have been hurt around horses, I can point to something foolish I did that led to the incident, and we'll address that concept later when we talk about improving your safety awareness.

case study

A brush with fear

It was feeding time at the farm and the horses were particularly anxious, when I walked into a pen full of yearling Thoroughbred fillies with a bucket of grain in each hand (stupid thing 1). Then I proceeded to the feed trough with all four fillies directly behind me (stupid thing 2). As luck would have it, the most dominant one was at the back of the line, where she emphatically did not want to be, and a series of chain reaction rump-bitings led to me being knocked down like a bowling pin and trampled by all four.

Fortunately, I did not sustain any serious injuries although I had a mouth full of mud and black and blue hoof prints all the way up my backside. Without question a fear memory was logged into my brain and to this day, some fifteen years later, the sound of horses moving behind me causes me to instinctively jump and spin around in self-defence. My pulse rate does not go up, I do not get frightened or shaky or short of breath; I just instinctively spin around, prepared for what might happen next.

> Fear memories are very real and very permanent, but they help to keep us from getting injured in the same way.

Fear memories are very real and very permanent, but they help to keep us from getting injured again in the same way. I'll never get run over by a horse from behind again; I just won't let that happen. We cannot erase any of our fear memories but we can train our conscious mind to over-ride the fear through training and discipline.

Post-traumatic fear

Sometimes a traumatic incident in other areas of your life may lead to an increased fear around horses. I recently heard from a woman who was the victim of a violent crime with no relationship whatsoever to horses, yet as a result she became paralyzed with fear when she went to the barn. Post-traumatic stress can manifest itself in many ways, but it is a real condition and one that takes time to heal. If you are dealing with a post-traumatic injury, it is critical to give your body and spirit the time it needs to heal before coming back to horse sports.

Characteristic of post-traumatic fear is a sense of loss and a high degree of frustration. A sense of grief can compound the fear because you have the feeling that you have lost something you once had, something very dear to you: the ability to ride unencumbered by fear. Sometimes people even fear that they have lost their riding ability and no longer have the skills they once had.

There is an equation that says:

$$\text{fear} + \text{grief} = \text{debilitation}$$

This means that you cannot deal with both of these emotions at once; it is simply too much for a person to handle. If you are suffering from this sense of loss and frustration in addition to your fear of horses, thinking that you no longer have the ability you once had before your injury, you must set aside your grief and deal with the fear first. You must have faith in the fact that you still have the same skill and ability that you had before your injury, and that this will come back to you as soon as you get control of the fear. You still have the same knowledge and skill with horses, you have just temporarily misplaced it. Once you have regained your confidence, you will ride like the wind once again.

The one and only person who has a right to determine when you are ready to come back to horse sports after an accident is you. Do not let anyone else influence this decision, and take all the time that you need to get there. Missing a year or two of riding never hurt anyone. One of the marvellous things about horse sports is that it is truly a life-long sport, so there is no need to be in a hurry. You'll know when you are ready to come back to riding, and at that time you will be much stronger, both physically and emotionally.

The nature of general anxiety

General anxiety is the fear that accumulates from the nasty 'what if' tricks our mind plays on us. General anxiety is very common among people struggling with a fear of horses, and the older we get, the more prone we are to this type of fear. Although occasionally seen in children, general anxiety is far more common in mature adults.

As we grow older, our life pressures tend to increase in direct proportion to the decrease in our body's ability to rebound from an injury. Life pressures contribute greatly to general anxiety, as sometimes we tend to feel the weight of the world on our shoulders. External pressures will exacerbate

Common 'What Ifs…'

- What if my horse runs away with me?

- What if my horse falls down on me and breaks my leg?

- What will happen to my job if I get hurt and can't go to work?

- Who will take the children to school?

- How will I pay my mortgage?

> There is only so much room in your mind for conscious thought, and if you can occupy that space with more productive thoughts, you can actually over-ride your general anxiety.

any fearful emotions so it is important to alleviate your stress as much as possible when you are ready to tackle your fear of horses. This will be an important part of your recovery plan, which we will come to later in this chapter.

It is a sad fact of nature that just when the wisdom of age has made us smart enough to handle almost anything life throws at us, our bodies are beginning to betray us. When we were kids we could get knocked down and bounce back up without missing a lick. As we age, the smaller knocks keep us down for much longer and it is only natural to have increased anxiety over getting hurt; we simply don't have the regenerative powers we once had.

The bad news is that general anxiety can cause our brain to spin totally out of control and can pollute our mind with outrageously negative energy. The good news is that we have the ability to control the thoughts in our mind and discipline ourselves to generate positive thoughts, thereby replacing and eliminating the negative ones.

General anxiety can have a very negative affect when it comes to dealing with your fear of horses, but you can learn, with practice and discipline, to replace those negative thoughts and focus on the positive outcome. There is only so much room in your mind for conscious thought, and if you can occupy that space with more productive thoughts, you can actually over-ride your general anxiety.

Many people struggling with fear, whether it is a fear of horses or from other areas of life, are dealing with both post-traumatic fear and general anxiety. No matter what the cause of your fear, it is important to analyze and understand its origins, and to look at the emotion objectively so that you can intellectualize the fear and develop a plan to counteract it.

A plan for recovery

Once you have analyzed, understood and intellectualized your fear and the symptoms manifested in your body, it is time to develop your management plan.

I always hesitate to use the term 'overcome your fear' because I feel it is a bit unrealistic. Fear memories cannot be erased, but they can be over-ridden with training. Because I work with fearful riders, I constantly coach them to step outside themselves and take an objective look at their emotions. By identifying the initial onset and the symptoms of fear, they can then take positive actions to manage it, rather than let the emotion take control.

Distinguish between stress and recovery

Before you begin to develop a plan to manage your fear, it is important for you to understand the difference between stress and recovery. Stress is the giving away of energy and recovery is the replenishment of it. The causes of stress and the methods of recovery will be different for each of us and so a sound understanding of your personal needs, including knowledge of when you are giving away and replenishing your energy, will help you to make a plan for coping with your fear.

For myself, I know that I need time alone in total quiet to replenish my stores of energy. I lead a very public life, on the road from forty to forty-five weeks a year, teaching clinics or giving seminars at horse fairs and conferences. Between sessions I am always happy to talk to horse owners one-to-one to help them resolve their horse issues or to listen to their horse stories. Although I am totally at ease standing up in front of a crowd of hundreds or thousands of people and in fact am energized by it, when I am talking to people individually, I know that I am being drained of energy.

As it turns out, I am an extreme introvert in personality although I am

Stress is the giving away of energy and recovery is the replenishment of it.

leading a life that most extroverts would thrive on. An introvert is someone who gains energy from being alone whereas an extrovert gains energy from being with others. I love working with people and horses but I know that at the end of the day I need some downtime, some time to be alone and replenish my energy. I must confess that sometimes at a particularly hectic horse fair, I escape to the ladies' room and lock myself in a cubicle for a few minutes to recoup my strength. My personal needs may be somewhat peculiar, but the important matter is that I know when I am being depleted of energy and what I need to do to replenish my stores.

Identify your own causes of stress and recovery

It is important for you to spend some time thinking about what causes you to give away your energy and what replenishes it; for each of us it will be different. Perhaps your job invigorates you, for example, or perhaps it drains you. The following table suggests examples of stress and recovery, but the permutations are endless.

It is important to recognize when you are stressing and giving away your energy, and to know what you have to do to replenish it and recover. Most importantly, when you are ready to take on this fear of horses, you need to begin with a full store of energy and come to it with as little built-up stress as possible.

Typical stress and recovery situations

Stress	Recovery
The giving away of energy	The replenishing of energy
For example:	For example:
• demands of family	• personal 'quiet' time
• job	• hobbies
• daily routine	• socializing
• other people	• rest

Making your plan

Before you can develop a recovery plan you need to identify exactly where your comfort level is and where it ends. Again, for each of us this will be different. Some people struggling with fear issues around horses are perfectly fine on the ground around them, but once in the saddle things change. For others, their comfort level is in the saddle and working on the ground is challenging. Some are fine at the walk and trot but even the mere thought of cantering makes them nauseous, whereas others are comfortable in the ring but scared to tears on the trail.

Identify your comfort zone

Your plan for recovery will involve spending lots of time within your comfort zone and taking small ventures outside of it for an occasional challenge, always returning to the comfort zone as needed. Before this plan can be made or executed, you must identify your personal comfort zone. It includes everything that you are confident and comfortable doing around horses and ends at the exact moment you feel the symptoms of fear begin to surface.

As you set about your routine tasks around the horse, pay close attention to your body and emotions, keeping in mind the symptoms of fear described earlier. Pay very close attention to your biofeedback because it is important you identify the precise moment at which you begin to feel your fear. That is the moment when you have just left your comfort zone. For instance, perhaps you arrive at the yard feeling good, you can go to your horse's stable and catch and halter him without stressing. You can manage him from the ground, groom him and clean out his feet without any fear or nervousness. But the moment you walk into the tack room to collect his saddle, you feel the butterflies start to flutter in your stomach. You have just left your comfort zone. This is important information to have as you set out to design your plan for recovery.

> Pay very close attention to your biofeedback because it is important you identify the precise moment at which you begin to feel your fear.

Extend your comfort zone

Your plan to learn to manage your fear will involve expanding your comfort zone, slowly but surely. Once you have a clear idea of where you are comfortable around horses and where that zone ends, you can plan to give yourself small challenges outside of it. With the example above, you should spend all the time you need going to the stable, getting your horse out, grooming him, cleaning his feet and then putting him away. When you are ready for your first small challenge, you will go to the stable, get him out, groom him, saddle him, then unsaddle and put him away again, repeating this pattern until retrieving your saddle from the tack room and saddling your horse no longer gives you butterflies. You have now expanded your comfort zone.

The next step in this plan might be to saddle your horse, take him to the arena to lunge him, then unsaddle and put him away. Again, spend as much time as you need until lungeing your saddled horse does not cause nervousness and your comfort zone has once again expanded. You might then lunge the horse and even mount, then dismount and return him to his stable. After you have expanded your comfort zone this far, your small challenges could grow to walking once around the arena and increasing the time and distance on each future occasion.

It is essential to make only small ventures outside your comfort zone and to return to the security of it to build confidence whenever necessary.

Take as long as you need

Another critical component of your recovery plan is that you have an open-ended time frame and that no one determines when you are ready for a challenge but you. Sometimes it helps to have a supportive friend or instructor to gently push you a little along the way, but it is important for you to know that you are the one in control and you will only move forward when you are ready. If it takes a year until you can saddle your horse without butterflies, who cares? Spend all the time you need and you'll know when you are ready for another challenge because you will be bored with the comfort zone you are in.

Share in your recovery

It may be helpful to share your plan with someone and to have some company and support as you venture down this path. Perhaps a partner, a riding companion or an instructor would be interested in hearing about your plan and of your little successes along the way.

Always remember to celebrate your successes and to make a note of every accomplishment. So often I see people in clinics who make tremendous progress, but then belittle their own progress by saying things like, 'Well, it took me long enough,' or 'I just wish I could have done more'. You need to make a point of celebrating every small achievement and sharing it with someone. At the same time, you must expect that there may be some minor setbacks along the way but don't let them discourage you too much. Accept that this is a normal part of the process, revert back to your comfort zone and know that more progress will come.

> Your family, your health, your career and your faith should rank higher on your priority list than riding.

Summary of your recovery plan

○ Identify your comfort zone.

○ Extend your comfort zone - slowly but surely.

○ Increase the size of your challenges.

○ Be prepared to stay below your comfort zone when necessary.

○ Have an open-ended timescale.

○ Share your plan with a trusted friend.

○ Celebrate your successes, no matter how small.

○ Be prepared for minor setbacks, but don't be discouraged.

Examine your life priorities

There are other factors in your life that may affect the success of your recovery plan.

First and foremost is to make sure you have your life priorities in order. If you stop to think about it, there are probably quite a few things more important in your life than riding horses. Your family, your health, your career, your values, and perhaps your faith should rank higher on your priority list than riding. When you put it all into perspective, you'll realize that your fear of horses is a minor thing and by considering your life priorities, you may find that riding is relatively unimportant. Sometimes, putting things into perspective will take the pressure off you enough to help ease your fear and lead to greater success.

Define your purpose

Defining purpose in your pursuit is also very important as purpose leads to courage. Although this can be difficult to do, you need to spend some time in deep introspection to determine exactly what it is. Ask yourself, for example:

- Why is it important to overcome this fear of riding?
- To whom is it important?
- Is it because I have a strong passion and desire to be with the horse or is it because someone else wants me to do it?
- Is it because I know the joy of riding like the wind or is it because of someone else's expectations?

Discovering your true purpose in horse sports can be very illuminating and might possibly lead you to the discovery that riding is not something you are doing for yourself. If this is the case and you are really going about this whole thing because of someone else's desire and purpose, you may need to reconsider. Horse sports are much too difficult and complicated to do for someone else. On the other hand, if after some serious introspection you discover it is a true passion and a lifetime goal, then this should give you greater courage. Recalling your true purpose when the going gets rough can help you reach down and discover some courage you didn't even know you had.

A classic example of how purpose leads to courage can be seen in the history of the United States Military. During World War II, hundreds of thousands of American soldiers lost their lives fighting a despicable tyrant who was known and understood to be the epitome of evil. They walked into the face of death fearlessly because they had purpose. On the other hand, during the Vietnam War, American soldiers were fighting in a war they did not comprehend, against an enemy that was unknown. Once again, thousands of soldiers lost their lives but for a cause they did not understand. There was a high desertion rate and the mental anguish the soldiers faced is still in evidence today. Purpose leads to courage, whether it is in battle or in horse sports.

> It is vital to make sure that there
> is fun and passion in what you do.
> After all, you didn't get into horses
> to create more stress in your life.

Ensure there is fun and passion

It is vital to make sure that there is fun and passion in what you do. Life is too short, and being involved with horses is too hard if these are absent. After all, you didn't get into horse sports to create even more stress in your life. I have followed my own passion for horses my entire life and I can tell you that I did not get into this business because of the money! Much to my surprise, however, I woke up a number of years ago to discover that I had totally lost the zest for what I did; I was actually starting to fantasize about having a nine-to-five job, working in an office under fluorescent lights.

How could I have lost my passion after pursuing a dream my whole life? With some serious introspection I discovered it had not actually gone but was just temporarily misplaced. I set out to rediscover it by spending more time riding my own horse instead of always riding someone else's, by attending some riding clinics for myself, and spending more time with training horses, which is where my true love lies. The point is that we have to make sure we keep in touch with our passion, and nurture it and feed it along the way. Without it, there is little point.

Look after yourself

Eating right and sleeping well are also essential factors in the success of your recovery plan. Chemistry is definitely a part of a calm focus; loading up on caffeine and sugar right before your head for the stable could have a negative effect on your nerves. Being well rested and rejuvenated before you accept a challenge will give you greater confidence. There is an old saying, 'Exhaustion makes cowards of us all'.

One other consideration that will lead to greater success with your recovery plan is to get in better shape. This does not mean that you have to become a strapping bodybuilder, but making an effort to improve your fitness will give you greater confidence – and I can prove it to you.

Have you ever, at any point in your life, made a commitment to lose weight or get in better shape? Most of us have at some time or another; usually it coincides with a New Year's resolution. So, as a part of this commitment, let's say you decide to walk around the block every morning. In keeping with your plan, you head out the next day, bright and early, for a brisk walk. When you get back, do you feel better? Of course you do, because you have made an effort to improve yourself. Are you any more fit than when you woke up that morning? Of course not, but making the effort made you feel better about yourself and that, in turn, leads to greater confidence. So make this commitment, in some small way, to improve your fitness and not only will it help with your recovery plan, there is the added bonus of improving your health.

hold the thought

Make a commitment, in some small way, to improve your fitness and not only will it help with your recovery plan, there is the added bonus of improving your health.

Faking it!

Another major component of managing your fear around horses and having success with your recovery plan is to learn some important acting skills that will help disguise and thus diminish your fear.

There are some specific skills you can acquire to control your breathing, your focus and your heart rate in order to dupe your mind and body into believing you are not afraid.

Your mind, body and spirit, the mental, the physical and the emotional, are all hopelessly connected. You cannot isolate any one of these parts of your being, and each one has an effect on the others. Thus, if you can learn to exert control over your mind and your body, it will have an effect on your spirit or your emotions.

Two of the most important physical skills for overcoming the emotion of fear are being able to control your breathing and keep your eyes focused.

Take control of your breathing

Your breathing is one of the very first things to change in the physical chain reactions that occur in your body when you become frightened. Think about what happens physiologically when your flight-or-fight response is triggered. The very first physical reaction is a sharp, sudden inhale, which causes the adrenalin rush that increases your heart rate and blood pressure in order to pump more oxygen to your muscles. On the other hand, what happens to your breathing when you finally relax? A long, deep sigh or exhale rids your body of the built-up carbon monoxide and cues it to unwind and let down its guard.

Learning to control your breathing can help hold off the other physical reactions of fear in your body. And because your mind, body and spirit are entwined, it will reduce the fear in your mind and spirit as well. Through breathing deeply, by filling your lungs fully from the bottom up and emptying them from the top downwards, you can actually learn to control your heart rate. Practise this skill outside of riding any time you have a start or feel your anxiety increase, and try slowing your heart rate through it. You do not have to be a yoga guru to master this skill; anyone can do it, but it does take practice.

Natural focus

Your eyes are the windows to your soul and another physiological reaction in your body to the emotion of fear is that they lose focus and shut down. This allows your mind to be polluted with negative thoughts or even panic. Learn to keep your eyes up and focused on things in your environment, taking in as much detail as possible. Notice people, things, colours, movements and reactions, and think about them as your eyes absorb the information.

By keeping your eyes active, focused and taking in such information, two things will happen to alleviate your fear. Firstly, your body will not kick into the downward spiral of physical reactions caused by fear because in keeping your eyes focused, you will fool it into confidence. Secondly, by absorbing the information of your environment, your mind will be filled with positive thoughts, leaving no room for the negative ideas that pollute your mind when fear takes over.

Practise breathing abdominally and keeping your eyes focused when you are in situations that may cause you to be fearful. These two skills alone can do more to help you learn to manage your fear of horses than anything else I know. A very popular equine publication in the United States, *Western Horseman*, did an article on a fear management clinic that I ran, in which they featured each participant individually. A couple of years later they did a follow-up piece to see what progress each individual had made in dealing with their fear of horses.

One of the questions asked to each person was, 'What skill did you learn in the clinic that has helped you the most in the past two years?' A majority

> If you display the body language of a strong and confident leader, your horse will accept your authority.

of the riders mentioned that learning to control their breathing and their eyes had significant impact on their ability to manage their fear. Another interesting note from this follow-up article is that while almost all of the participants reported an occasional setback, they had all made tremendous strides in managing their fear by simply enacting a recovery plan and developing their acting skills.

Know your body language

In addition to controlling your eyes and your breathing, it is important to employ some other valuable acting skills. Controlling your body language will go a long way to convince both your mind and your horse that you are confident. The body language of a confident person is indicated by an erect posture, alert eyes, slow breathing and square shoulders. Conversely, a person who lacks confidence or is frightened will look down with unfocused eyes, rounded shoulders, shallow breathing and will fidget excessively.

Be aware of your body language and the message it is sending to your horse. This is one reason why horses can size up humans so effectively and will act differently around different people. If you display the body language of a strong and confident leader, your horse will accept your authority. On the other hand, if your body language indicates weakness and a lack of confidence, your horse may become frightened or may decide that he is better qualified to be the leader and start issuing orders to you.

No matter how you feel on the inside, it is important never to show your weakness on the outside. This old axiom has been around a long time and is frequently applied to the corporate world and to athletic competitors, but it also plays a significant role when dealing with horses. Not only will your horse respond better to a confident demeanour but it will have a positive effect on your mind and spirit as well. Remember that the mind, body and spirit are all connected: if our bodies are exuding confidence, our mind and spirit will follow.

Along these lines, some people I have dealt with in clinics have benefited from adopting the attitude, 'Give me more, I can take it!' This frame of mind encourages a certain amount of bravado that will give you confidence. It's not that you want to expose yourself to unnecessary risk but it is the attitude that counts. The 'I can take whatever you dish out' attitude will prompt your body language and therefore your psyche into feeling confident.

Play an internal video

One final exercise that will help you to increase your confidence is to play an internal video in your mind. Identify a rider who epitomizes the ultimate horseman to you; a rider you would be happy to resemble. Maybe it's your trainer, a friend or companion, or even an Olympic equestrian. Study this rider, either in person or by watching videos of him or her ride until you have the image burned into your brain. Memorize every detail, from the way they hold the reins and sit in the saddle to the way they put a foot in the stirrup and pet the horse.

When you are ready to get on your horse and ride, play the video in your mind and imagine you are that rider. This is a very valuable exercise and often professional athletes are coached to do the same thing. Have a picture playing in your mind of the most positive outcome you can imagine and you'll be surprised how your body will follow. By filling your thoughts with a positive image, there is little room left in your brain for the negative 'what if' thoughts that lead you into the black hole of fear.

By employing these tactics, your mind, body and spirit will be convinced that there is no reason to be frightened and you will gain confidence. At the same time, your horse will feel more secure in your leadership.

Have a picture playing in your mind of the most positive outcome you can imagine and you'll be surprised how your body will follow.

Vital acting skills needed for managing fear

- ○ Practise deep abdominal breathing.
- ○ Keep your eyes focused and taking in information from your environment.
- ○ Get control of your body language and display a confident demeanour.
- ○ Adopt the 'Give me more, I can take it' attitude.
- ○ Play an internal video of a rider you want to resemble.

Polish your horsemanship and safety skills

A huge factor in gaining confidence around horses is to improve your knowledge of horse behaviour in order to increase your riding skill and improve your safety habits.

The more you know and understand about horse behaviour, the safer you will be around horses. Understanding herd hierarchy and the communicative behaviours of horses will improve your relationship with your horse and thus increase confidence in you both.

Understanding herd dynamics

Horses are prey animals and everything about their physiology and behaviour is based on this fact. Their keen senses, their flight instinct and their herd mentality are important elements of survival. As highly evolved predators ourselves, we have difficulty relating to the fact that horses are concerned for their survival during every waking moment. Often, behaviour that we think of as 'stupid' in a horse is really a factor of its strong survival instinct.

Horses are also herd animals and do not survive in solitary situations, being dependent on the safety of the herd. Even in the wild, the young stallions driven away from the main herd will find bachelor groups to join up with for security. Much of what we know about horse behaviour stems from the society that exists within the herd framework.

You don't have to be around horses for long to discover that there is a certain order within the herd: what is commonly referred to as the pecking order, the equine behaviourists refer to as a 'linear hierarchy'. The definition of this is that each individual in the herd is either dominant over, or subordinate to, every other individual. In other words, there is no equality in the herd.

Since horses have no way of understanding human behaviour, it is

> It is helpful to know where your
> horse fits into the pecking order…
> a very alpha horse can be
> challenging to many riders…

incumbent upon us to understand their behaviour and interact with them in a way they can comprehend. Keeping that in mind, you need to consider you and your horse to be a herd of two. Due to the nature of the herd, you now have two choices: you can be the dominant member or the subordinate member. Hopefully, we are all clear on the fact that we want to be dominant and not be taking orders from an animal that at any moment can transform into a thousand-pound scared rabbit!

What is not always so clear to us humans is what factors determine dominance and subordinance.

Dominance and subordinance

Two factors determine dominance within the herd: resources and space. Firstly, the dominant horse always controls the resources of the herd: anything of value and generally including food, water and perhaps shelter. One of the easiest ways to determine the pecking order in any particular herd is to observe the horses at feeding time. The dominant animal, technically referred to as the 'alpha individual' and sometimes called the 'boss mare', will always eat first, followed by the second most dominant and so forth. The last horse to eat is at the bottom of the pecking order and is referred to as the 'omega individual'.

Even in a domestic herd, it is helpful to know where your horse fits into the pecking order, to know if he is naturally dominant, naturally subordinate or somewhere in the middle. A very alpha horse can be challenging to many riders, especially if they are struggling with fear and confidence issues. Generally speaking, a horse somewhere in the middle of the pecking order is more desirable.

The second factor in determining dominance in the herd is the issue of space, and one at which we humans often fail. The dominant horse controls the space of the subordinate horse; this fact of herd behaviour can be easily observed by watching any group of horses for just a few minutes. When a dominant horse moves toward a subordinate, the subordinate horse moves an equal distance away. If it doesn't, it is very likely to be bitten. Like humans, horses have their own personal space and for each individual, that space varies. A subordinate horse will never move into the space of a dominant one. Furthermore, the subordinate horse is constantly aware of where the dominant horse is and what it is doing.

Whenever a new horse is introduced into the herd there is a period of flux until the newcomer finds his rightful place in the pecking order. At first the new horse will be driven away by dominant herd mates, as if to say, 'We do not want you in our herd, go away.' The new horse knows that his very survival is dependent upon being accepted, so he will come back again and again, asking for acceptance, only to be chased away.

Eventually the newcomer will stand on the edge of the herd, facing the dominant horse and drop his head all the way to the ground in the ultimate act of contrition as if to beg, 'Please let me in; I'll do anything to be accepted.' At this point, the dominant horse will usually turn her back and walk away, allowing the new horse to come into the fold. As time goes by, he will gradually work his way up the pecking order until he finds his rightful place by determining whose space he can control and from whom he can take away food.

A thorough understanding of herd hierarchy has important implications for the way you interact with and handle horses. In many, if not most, of the relationships I see between a horse and human on the amateur level, the horse is dominant and clearly in charge. In most instances this is because the human has not been an adequate leader for the horse and with a lack of leadership and authority, the horse has stepped into the dominant role to fill the void. There are many minor factors that can erode your relationship with your horse, and when combined, these small faults can turn into a major failure.

A thorough understanding of herd hierarchy has important implications for the way you interact with horses.

The horse's perspective

Keeping in mind that the dominant horse controls the resources and the space of his subordinates, making mistakes along these lines can lead to an unsatisfactory relationship with him. Like many trainers, I do not approve of hand-feeding treats to horses because, more often than not, the practice leads to spoiled and disrespectful behaviour, although not for the reasons that most people think. It is a common belief that hand-feeding is something you shouldn't do because it causes a horse to bite, encouraging him to mistake your hand for a titbit.

If you look at this from the horse's point of view, however, it will become clear why hand-feeding really leads to problems. First of all, when you hand over the treat to a horse, you are essentially giving him your food. He has no way of knowing it is a 'horse treat' and that you wouldn't eat it even if you were hungry. All he knows is that it is food and that he is taking it away from you. Since the dominant horse in the herd controls the resources, you have just convinced your horse that he is dominant. This problem will not occur the very first time you give the treat, but in subsequent feedings. Once he comes to expect it and even to 'ask' for it, he comes to believe he is taking away your food.

Secondly, when a horse approaches you to take the treat, he is moving into your space and putting his lips on you. These are two actions that a subordinate horse would never take towards a dominant animal. If the behaviour progresses to the horse pushing into your space and nudging, sniffing and even head butting for the titbit, he has become dominant and disrespectful. If this is the case, when you hand over the treat, you not only reward his disrespectful behaviour, but also show him that he now controls the resources.

The hand-fed horse does not begin to bite because he mistakes your finger for a carrot, although that can certainly happen if you are careless. It is actually the act of letting a horse put his lips on you that leads to biting behaviour. Biting is the most aggressive behaviour seen in horses and it develops from progressive behaviours associated with dominance. The progression starts with 'lipping' (when a horse is allowed to put his lips on you), leads to nipping and finally develops into biting. Lipping can start as a playful experiment where a horse tests his boundaries by putting his muzzle on you and nuzzling. If this goes unchecked, the horse will begin to nip, taking a small pinch of skin between his lips but typically backing off because he knows he has done something wrong. If nipping is then allowed to go unchallenged, it will lead to aggressive biting, a very dangerous and malicious behaviour.

How you interact with your horse on a day-to-day and even minute-to-minute basis will determine the type of relationship you have with him. Understanding the factors that lead to dominance and subordinance, and treating your horse like a horse rather than a human, will lead to the ideal relationship with him in which you are the leader and he is the obedient, respectful follower.

The benefits of groundwork

Learning to do groundwork is another highly effective way to establish the leader-follower relationship and to gain confidence around the horse.

In my fear management clinics we spend a lot of time doing groundwork so that each handler learns to control the horse's entire body, the nose, shoulder, feet and hip, simply through the use of hand gestures and body language; through mental control and not the physical control achieved with ropes and restraints. Relationship training in this way builds in two basic stages.

The first stage occurs in the round pen, where we learn to drive the horse away from us, control his direction and control his speed, gain his focus,

> Develop a line of communication in which the horse is looking to you for directives as his leader.

respect and trust, and finally to develop a line of communication in which the horse is looking to us for directives as his leader. The second stage introduces lead-line work, practised with a rope halter and a 4 to 5 metre training rope. Through the lead-line work we teach the horse to respect our space and to be obedient and mannerly. We'll work on teaching the horse to stand quietly upon our request and not move a foot unless asked; to keep his nose in front of his chest and remain focused on us; to lead quietly at our side moving exactly as we move, step for step, neither lagging behind, getting in front or dragging us where he wants to go; to yield his shoulder and hip and disengage the hindquarters (crossing his hindlegs in an act of submission); and finally to work in a circle around us at the speed we ask of him and changing directions with a simple hand signal.

Achieving this type of relationship with your horse will give you satisfaction and a sense of fulfilment, and will also increase your confidence, both from the ground and in the saddle as you gain a sense of control and develop a clear line of communication with him.

Stage 1: Working in a round pen

Learn how to:
• Drive the horse away from you
• Control his direction and speed
• Gain his focus, respect and trust
• Develop a line of communication in which the horse is looking to you for directives

Teach your horse to:
• Respect your space and to be obedient and mannerly

Stage 2: Working with a 4 to 5 metre rope

• Stand quietly upon your request and not move a foot unless asked
• Keep his nose in front of his chest and remain focused on you
• Lead quietly at your side
• Disengage the hindquarters
• Work in a circle at different speeds and changing direction

Safety skills

In addition to understanding the nature and behaviour of the horse, it is also important to recognize where the danger zones are around him. Although flight is always the first choice when it comes to avoiding danger, if forced to fight, he has a highly effective arsenal at his disposal. He has three ways to defend himself, and in order of severity can bite, strike or kick.

As I have already said, biting is the most aggressive and deadly behaviour in horses and when they fight to kill in the wild, they kill with a bite to the jugular. That is why you will often see teeth marks around a male horse's throat when he has been sparring with other geldings or stallions. Horses that bite aggressively are dangerous animals, and should be handled and rehabilitated by only the most experienced of horsemen.

Striking is another aggressive fighting behaviour and it occurs when a horse strikes out with a front leg. It is particularly hazardous because the animal can rear and strike, coming down on its enemy with tremendous force. Striking can be bullet fast and will sometimes occur when a horse has a sharp or sudden pain in his head, such as a bee sting.

Kicking is the least severe defensive mechanism of the horse, even though it is the one we think about the most. Horses usually kick when being attacked from behind and the action is actually a less aggressive behaviour. If you observe horses in the herd, you will most often see kicking when a dominant horse attacks a subordinate and the subordinate will kick and run away. Kicking buys the horse a little time in order to make a hasty retreat. Although sometimes horses kick aggressively, usually with both hind feet in order to back down a challenger, most of the time it is defensive in nature. People are most likely to be kicked when approaching the horse from behind or when doing something that makes him feel as if he is being attacked.

Understanding these aggressive and defensive behaviours, and how the horse moves when he is displaying one of them, will help keep you much safer. It is interesting to note that two of the three occur in the front end of

Understanding aggressive and defensive behaviours, and how the horse moves when he is displaying them, will help keep you much safer.

the horse, even though we tend to focus on staying away from the rear. It is important to remember, however, that a horse can also kick forward and to the side with his hind leg.

Safety habits

You should always be conscious of where the danger zones are around the horse and make an effort to stay out of the way or minimize the risk. An example of being in such a zone without recognizing it occurs when you are cleaning out a front foot. As you bend down to pick up the hoof, your head can easily come into the kick zone since the horse can reach almost all the way up to his front legs with the hind foot. Whenever you have cause to bend down underneath a horse, you should always face forward so that your rear end, instead of your head, is in the kick zone.

It is a good idea to wear a helmet, approved and tested for equestrian use, at all times when you are working around horses, not just when you are riding. Head injuries represent a significant percentage of horse-related injuries, and protecting your biggest asset, your brain, is a good idea.

There are many good safety habits you can adopt, and each one will help protect you and thus improve your confidence. Not ducking under the horse's head when he is tied, never wrapping the lead rope around your wrist but folding it into your hand, wearing appropriate footwear and other protective equipment, are all important safety rules to follow.

Improve your riding skills

Improving your riding skill is another important factor in developing greater confidence. Working to improve your balance on the horse, your ability to move rhythmically with him and the ability to use your natural aids (your seat, legs, hands and voice) in a more effective manner will make you a better rider.

It is often helpful to take lessons on a gentle, proven schoolmaster, allowing you to work on improving your personal riding skills before tackling your own horse. Finding a qualified, effective and understanding instructor who can both assist you to improve your riding skill as well as support your plan for managing your fear of horses is a must-have. They also need to be someone with whom you can personally connect.

In fear-management clinics we focus on improving the balanced position of ear-shoulder-hip-heel alignment, on learning to keep joints and muscles loose and relaxed in order to better absorb the motion of the horse rather than bounce on his back, and to use the seat, legs and hands in an effective and coordinated manner to communicate with him. I also teach riders two important skills for gaining better control of a fractious horse: the pulley rein and the one-rein stop.

The pulley rein

The pulley rein is an emergency stopping manoeuvre applied when the horse is bucking or bolting. When applied correctly, it will stop any horse dead in its tracks. It is executed by shortening one rein as tight as you can and pushing your knuckles into the crest of the horse's neck. It is important that your hand is braced and centred on his neck, and not floating free. You then slide your other hand down the second rein as far forward as you can and pull straight

> Consider taking lessons on a gentle, proven schoolmaster to improve your personal riding skills before tackling your own horse.

back and up with all your weight. Since the first rein is locked and braced, it is preventing your horse's head from turning so the pull on the second rein creates a lot of pressure on his mouth.

If the pulley rein is executed correctly, you can stop a runaway horse on its nose. This is far preferable to pulling the out-of-control horse into a circle, since that may cause him to lose his footing and fall. The technique does require some practice and the practice can be very hard on your horse so many instructors do not like to teach this form of emergency stop. However, when you are out of control, it is a great tool to have in your bag of tricks and it can be very useful for slowing down a strong horse, with a little pulley action every few strides, followed by a release. You can use it with your half halt.

One of the very worst things you can do when trying to slow down or stop a horse is pull back on both reins at the same time. This will almost always make him stiffen his neck and lock his jaw, and may also pull you up and out of the saddle, even right over his ears. Pulling on both reins continuously will often cause the horse to 'run through the bridle', and the harder you pull, the faster he will go. Horses are far more responsive to using the reins alternately, which is far more likely to keep them soft in the neck and flexing at the poll. Unfortunately, most people have been taught to stop by pulling back on both reins, yet using one is much more effective.

The one-rein stop

The other technique I would therefore teach for better control is a one-rein stop or a disengagement of the hindquarters. This is done as a training process at slow speeds, before the horse gets out of control. You execute the one-rein stop by picking up one rein, and one rein only, and lifting it up towards your belly button or opposite shoulder. It is an upward, diagonal pull on the rein, not a backwards tug, and it is critical that the other rein is completely loose.

This rein aid will turn the horse's nose up and towards you, and as he arcs throughout the length of his body the turn will cause him to disengage, or cross his hind legs. Almost any rider is capable of feeling the horse's hips bend as he begins to disengage the hindquarters.

Disengagement will help you control the horse in two ways: speed and subordinance. When the horse crosses his hind legs in disengagement, he ceases all forward motion. As you slowly pick up on the one rein, wait until you feel the horse's back and hip bend (that is when he is crossing his hind legs), then release the rein suddenly and completely, and he should stop. If not, just reapply the aid, but be sure to release as soon as you feel the horse even begin to slow down. It should be a slow and steady lift of the rein and an instantaneous release when you feel the horse's momentum affected. You should alternate between the right and left reins, or the inside and outside rein, so you are not influencing just one side of the horse or getting him into a habit. The one-rein stop will cause your horse to turn at first, but with practice and a timely release, he will go straight and stop.

Disengagement of the hindquarters occurs any time the horse crosses his hind legs, one in front of the other, and causes submissiveness in his mind because it takes away his ability to flee. It is a natural behaviour occasionally seen in neo-natal foals (foals under one month of age). When the mother disciplines an unruly foal, it will sometimes cross its hind legs in contrition. As the foal matures, the behaviour no longer occurs voluntarily but we can ask the horse to disengage, either from the ground or from the saddle, and it will cause him to be more submissive, even if only for a moment.

Once the horse is trained for the one-rein stop, you can stop him at any time with just a lift of one rein. Any time he loses his focus or becomes fractious, you should immediately disengage his hindquarters until his focus comes back to you. The pulley rein and one-rein stop are important skills to learn to help you have better control and build your confidence at the same time.

Pick the right company

It is also important to choose your company wisely when riding in a group.

Not all riders are aware of proper riding etiquette or have adequate control of their mounts. Make sure that any group you ride with has established rules and that all riders are in agreement as to the level of difficulty and speed of the ride. Have an agreement on what gaits you will use and who will give the cue to the group to go and stop. Make sure everyone's horse is well trained and reliable, since horses will tend to act like the others around them. Finally, make sure you are riding in an area that someone in the group is familiar with, and that you have the means for emergency contact, should it become necessary.

Learning to cope with a fear of horses and of riding requires a multi-faceted approach. The summary on the following page will give you a sound checklist as you make and execute your plan.

Attacking your fear of horses on all of these levels will give you great success. Remember, fear is a perfectly normal emotion and there is nothing wrong with you for feeling it. By approaching your fear you will gain control over the emotion and get back to enjoying your horse more than you ever imagined. Always have faith in the positive outcome.

○ First, understand the origins of your fear and its physical effect. Develop the ability to look at this emotion objectively.

○ Make a plan for recovery, identify your comfort zones and accept small challenges; have an open-ended time frame to enact your plan, be sure to share it with someone else and celebrate your successes along the way.

○ Put your life priorities in order and make sure that you aren't assigning a greater importance to this minor issue. Find your purpose with horses because purpose leads to courage.

○ Take good care of yourself; eat right, sleep well, replenish your energy and make an effort to get in better shape.

○ Develop your acting skills so that you can fake it until you make it. Practise deep abdominal breathing to control your heart rate; learn to keep your eyes focused; adopt a positive attitude and make sure it shows in your body language; play an internal video of your favourite rider and have the mental discipline to think positive thoughts.

○ Improve your knowledge of horse behaviour and your ability to control horses from the ground. Communicate with them effectively in a language they understand.

○ Improve your riding skills by taking lessons on a trained and reliable school horse from a qualified and empathetic instructor.

○ Most importantly, adopt safe practices around horses; wear your helmet always, be alert to potential danger and ride in good company.

2
Understanding the Horse

Abigail Hogg

'Abigail Hogg's approach is informed by the study of
horse psychology and physiology. She has a holistic
approach to horse training, considering all aspects of
the horse's life, and bases her teaching on a sound
understanding of how animals learn.
She believes that gaining an understanding of the
horse can boost a rider's confidence.'

Why they frighten us

The fear of horses is more common than we generally think. People can be afraid for many reasons and riders are not exempt from this fear. It is seldom talked about, however, as it can be embarrassing, holding us back from what we want to achieve and making us anxious about appearing foolish. But the fear of horses is a natural emotion and one that we can surmount. By taking steps to understand their nature and behaviour, and learning how to select the best horse for our purpose, it is possible to overcome fear.

Horses are scary because of their sheer physical capability. Their speed of movement and strength are essential to their survival and to the activities that we want to do with them. But this speed and strength can also be dangerous. In the wild, the horse has space to move and there are no fragile humans in the way. In domestication, the horse's space is restricted and we are often in his line of movement. Understandably, many people lose confidence due to a traumatic incident and this may escalate because as we get more tense and nervous, we increase the chances of further problems.

If we consider the potential for physical injury, it's not surprising we find horses frightening. To run through the list of possibilities, being bitten, kicked, trodden on, crushed, charged, head butted and thrown off are the obvious threats; however, people also fear being ignored, disobeyed and disliked. Add to this the fear of ridicule or disapproval from other humans and the fear of failure, whether in getting the correct canter lead or performing well in a competition, and we can see that horses may add up to being fairly frightening animals. Yet so many of us persist.

What are we dealing with?

Horses are large, strong animals and healthy caution is important when dealing with them. If they lived their lives without interference from humans, they would spend their time on the open plains searching for food and water, breeding,

hold the thought

Fear of horses is a natural emotion and one that need not spoil our enjoyment.

socializing, sheltering and resting. Occasionally, if they perceived there to be danger, they would run.

This is a different life to that of domestication. The horse kept by humans for the purpose of being used by humans is living in an alien world. He is forced into a close relationship with an animal that is not of the same species, that looks different, communicates differently and demands that he do things that are frankly quite bizarre. Not only that, but he often has to live in a way that prevents him spending his time in the way he has evolved to. His movement is restricted, his social life is restricted, his food is restricted and, to top it all, he is asked to carry or pull, to wear tack and clothing, to jump obstacles that he could go round and to tolerate noise and activity that he would prefer to run away from.

Yet perhaps the most difficult aspect of living with human beings is understanding what we are trying to say to him. As a species, we are not good at the type of communication horses use. We have speech. They have body language. In actual fact, we also read each other's body language, but we tend to take more notice of what is said and how it is said, than of body position. Horses exist as a member of a herd before they exist as individuals. They are tuned in to living with each other for every second of the day, constantly reading the signals given out by one another, signs so subtle that most people can't see, let alone understand them. We must be extremely difficult animals for a horse to figure out.

It is unlikely that horses think of us as carnivores or predators, as is sometimes suggested. If they were really worried about predators, they would be nervous wrecks every time the family dog or cat appeared. The fact is, horses are sensitive to novelty and change; anything unusual makes them cautious. Once they recognize that something is safe, they will relax and accept it. Sadly, there are many horses that at best see us as something to be tolerated and at worst are actually afraid of us, attitudes that arise because of their experiences of humans.

No need for fear

The good news is that horses have a great capacity for calm and the ability to get on with each other, both characteristics that they will generously extend to humans, if given the chance. Naturally, their entire life should take place as part of a complex set of relationships with other horses. When horses are studied, both in the wild and in domestic situations that mimic natural living conditions, it is found that over 80 per cent of their social interactions work to keep the group together. Even the remaining behaviour that isn't classed as cohesive is not necessarily divisive, but includes avoidance behaviour, such as moving away. It is possible to move away from another horse without dividing the group.

How does this help us reassess our attitude to horses? Well, it lets us know that, by nature, they're not out to get us. They are not trying to dominate us, show us who's boss, get one over on us, stamp on us, kick us, bite us, throw us on the floor or stomp on us. Yet we all know horses that do just these things, so we need to consider the reasons why. If we take a two-year-old that is familiar with humans and has been gently handled and well kept, we usually find that he is curious about us, willing to follow and a pleasure to be around. Horses that don't react in this way are usually those with absolutely no experience of humans – and so are frightened of the novelty – or those with a lot of experience.

Horses that are satisfied with their lives are generally calm and not aggressive. This applies to Thoroughbreds as much as to Shires. Biologically, it is not a good strategy to spend energy in moving unnecessarily or fighting with the members of your herd. The first activity takes precious time away from eating, and the second may leave you outside the group and susceptible to predators. Yet many horses live in a state of constant agitation, always moving, refusing to eat, pulling faces, threatening other horses, kicking the stable door, biting passers-by, and generally acting like dangerous animals. This behaviour will be familiar to most people but, if we stop and consider for a moment, we realize that this is a herbivorous prey animal we are talking about.

By nature, horses are not out to get us.
They are not trying to dominate us, show
us who is boss, get one over on us,
stamp on us or kick us.

The first step towards understanding how horses should be, and realizing that they are not intrinsically dangerous, is to spend time with a group of calm horses and see how they interact. Such groups are those that are well established, living outside with enough space and food not to need to compete.

Do horses intend to hurt us?

So why do we see horses that apparently want to eat human flesh or dump us in front of an oncoming truck? The answers may be found in the realities of domestic horses' lives: lifestyle, pain and poor training.

Lifestyle

In a natural environment a horse that is not happy with the situation he is in will leave. Domestic life blocks this course of action. An average stable for a horse is similar in proportion to a battery cage for a hen. It takes away space to flee so a horse that is agitated or frightened while in the stable cannot escape. Nor can a horse that is being held on a headcollar or bridle. This doesn't mean that he won't try. The human's reaction to this is to attempt to make him stand still. This is virtually impossible for the horse, an animal that runs from danger. Once the adrenalin is pumping, the only outlet is movement, yet the horse leaping around on the end of a lead rope is frightening and rightly so, because he can easily hurt us. Given the choice, once released from the restriction, he wouldn't choose to jump on our toes and shoulder charge us; he would just leave.

The physical restrictions we place on horses also prevent them fulfilling a natural need for movement, an innate part of their behaviour. Horses move most of the time because they need to travel to get food. Their rest periods are interspersed with movement; not for them eight hours sleep while it's dark. The mind and body are inseparable when it comes to this, so it isn't just a psychological need for movement we are dealing with. The horse's digestive system is designed to extract nutrition from large quantities of poor forage. His body is designed to be healthy by being outside and moving. The blood vessels in the horse's legs depend on the action of the hoof being pressed on to the ground to help pump the blood back up the leg, and this aids healing. Vitamin D is manufactured from the effect of sunlight on the skin. Horses need fresh air; those that have always lived outside rarely, if ever, suffer from flu or respiratory problems.

A lot of the behaviour that makes us fearful of horses is simply pent-up energy, which may arise from overfeeding and restriction but also because it's virtually impossible to give a domestic horse conditions that give him enough exercise, even if he is kept completely free-range. Too much energy may manifest itself as high spirits or it may be a build-up of violent energy because the horse is suffering from ongoing stress or is afraid. Either way, the outcome is not good for us; we aren't designed to be playmates for horses and an aggressive horse can be lethal.

Pain and discomfort

Many domestic horses are suffering from chronic pain. Unfortunately ongoing low-level pain is probably more common than we realize as even with sore backs or slight lameness, horses can continue working for many years. Some experts estimate that only 10 per cent of domestic horses are truly 100 per cent sound. Most horses stoically tolerate discomfort; however, some will always be unsettled and bothered. There is also the acute pain caused by a saddle that doesn't fit or

hold the thought

> Horses often clearly communicate that they are in pain. Humans often fail to recognize these messages.

discomfort in the mouth due to the bit or the rider's hand. The experience of pain may be manifested as irritation or even aggression towards people or other horses. It may also be shown in frantic activity.

Horses often clearly communicate that they are in pain. For example, a horse that doesn't want to be saddled is probably not just being awkward or lazy but is saying, in the only way he can, that he finds the saddle unpleasant. Humans often fail to recognize these messages however hard the horse works to speak our language. The horse that opens his mouth and raises his head in response to pressure on the bit will usually find himself with his head tied down by a martingale and his mouth clamped shut with a noseband. The idea that the bit may be wrong or the rider heavy-handed isn't usually considered. The horse that consistently refuses to jump may have problems with his legs or hooves that are not yet detectable, yet refusals make jumping nerve-racking for the rider; there's nothing worse than trying to ride confidently at a jump when there's a fifty-fifty chance that you'll be the only one who clears it. The point is that the horse's reaction to pain and discomfort becomes dangerous to us and increases our fear.

Misunderstanding and fear

A horse that doesn't understand what is wanted of him or is afraid will be dangerous. The natural reaction to escape will kick in and this escape is usually thwarted by the human. Once restricted, the horse's flight reaction becomes violent behaviour and is interpreted as fighting, though in reality the horse would simply run away if given the choice. Horses rarely attack humans but there are some that will, if pushed enough.

The anticipation of pain or fear will make a horse fearful and resistant. The horse that turns his rump towards a human who enters the stable is usually being defensive, but the human perceives this as a threat to kick, which on occasions it might be. The point is that both horse and human are afraid of each other. The horse can't change his attitude to the human, so the human must find ways to take away the horse's apprehension about the situation.

A horse that anticipates punishment will understandably try to get away. It's worth thinking for a moment how it must feel to be hit by someone who is actually sitting on your back and preventing you from escaping the beating.

Horses have moods too

When someone who doesn't know about horses approaches one, the first question is often, 'Will it kick?' I tend to look at the animal dozing on three legs and wonder how anyone could think he was about to kick. However, horses have a reputation for kicking (although more tend to bite than kick) and that resting hind leg could be read as a warning. A fact to remember is that fear can be reduced by learning to read the signals your horse is giving out. Horses are generally very clear in their signals. Body language is made up of a number of factors including body position, facial expression and quality of movement.

Relaxation or stress? Signs to look out for when assessing the mood of your horse

Relaxation/acceptance	Tension/stress
• low head	• head high
• relaxed mouth	• mouth tight
• licking and chewing – often a sign of relaxation after a period of tension	
• resting one foot	
• calm eyes	• eyes and ears in constant motion
• relaxed movements	• agitated movements
• not moving more than is necessary	• moving more than is necessary

It is important to learn to control our emotions and to present a picture of complete confidence to the horse.

When we ask horses to learn or perform, we are actually looking for a state of mind and body between relaxation and tension; in other words, arousal without tension. Staying safe means learning to recognize this state and being able to spot the indications that the horse is becoming tense and feeling stressed.

Two sides to the story

Horses are adept at reading mood in others.
This means that the attitude with which you approach a horse is important. If you've got ten minutes to get groomed and tacked up, and so rush up to your horse in a state of urgency, it is likely that he will respond badly. If you are feeling angry or short-tempered, your mood will have an effect on your horse and he will be less likely to be cooperative. Horses are highly tuned in to picking up alarm in each other. They recognize physical tension and read body posture and quality of movement, so that jerky movements, for example, will alarm them. They also use sound in specific ways, often subtly, for example when calling to a foal or courting.

This ability to read body language in each other is also applied to us, although with time, many horses become habituated to human heavy-handedness or fussiness and will ignore it. The same applies to talking. Horses can learn specific word cues, if taught and used consistently, but the babbling we tend to do at them means nothing. The effect on us is that if we say to a horse, 'Now you stand still and be a good boy,' subconsciously we tend to act as if we think he has been told once and will obey, and we are more likely to get annoyed when he doesn't. Of course, all the horse hears is another stream of random sound and, as far as he's concerned, he hasn't been given any instruction about whether to stand still or not.

In this scenario, we can see how differently horses perceive a situation to ourselves. Another example of where confusion can arise is when the human attempts to pick up the horse's foot. The following table illustrates how perceptions of this may differ, leading to a potentially frightening incident.

Picking up the horse's foot – two perspectives	
Horse	**Human**
• Preconceived idea that hooves are precious and not to be restricted in any way	• Preconceived idea that horses routinely kick
• Can't see what the human is doing to the hoof	• Can't see how the horse is reacting
• Uncomfortable to stand on three legs	• Uncomfortable to bend over and support the weight of the horse
• Every time horse moves the human leaps away, which is frightening	• Horse keeps moving, which is frightening

In considering the above scenario, we can picture an increasing level of nervousness as each party responds to the reactions of the other.

⊃ The horse raises his leg a little higher
⊃ The human lets go of the leg and leaps away
⊃ The leaping human startles the horse
⊃ The human gets more nervous
⊃ The human tentatively approaches the horse again
⊃ The horse reads all the signs of great caution in the human and becomes more worried
⊃ The human carefully picks up the foot again
⊃ The horse snatches his foot away and the human again leaps away in panic

Thus the situation escalates. Someone has to take control and say clearly, 'This is okay; there's nothing to worry about. I'll just hold your leg calmly here, you relax and it will all be fine.' It's not pleasant for a horse to be around another nervy being.

Training the horse

How do we train a horse? First, we have to be clear how horses (and all animals, including ourselves) learn, how we should use rewards and how not to abuse the horse in the belief that we are punishing him. Secondly, we have to know exactly what we want the horse to do; and thirdly, we have to understand that we need to break our training down into chunks that may be minute steps towards the final behaviour we are trying to teach. If we want to jump, we start with a single pole on the ground once the horse is balanced enough to carry a rider and understands the basic aids. We don't train a horse to jump by entering him in a class at a show. If he's having difficulty balancing with a rider on board and doesn't understand an aid to slow down but we start asking for jumping, we're heading for a problem.

We need also to be aware that horses are inadvertently trained to behave in certain ways. If you buy a horse that has been ridden by a fearless teenager, you may find that as soon as his hooves hit grass, he's ready to gallop. This is pretty scary if you're not ready to gallop yourself, but the horse is simply doing what he has learned. You can, however, train a horse to behave in a certain way that is not frightening to you. I have trained my horse to wait behind while other horses gallop ahead; I don't have to physically stop him from going but, instead, can actually wait with a loose rein until I say we go. This is a great asset when riding in a group but wanting to remain in control of your own pace. If your horse won't stand still to mount, then take the time to teach him by breaking down the act of mounting into stages. He may not be being naughty or refusing to let you mount, but may have been taught the opposite, to set off as soon as a toe is in the stirrup.

hold the thought

You can train a horse to behave in a certain way that is not frightening to you.

Making him safe

Much of the training we do with a horse is implicitly about making him safe to ride and handle. However it is worth spending extra time on elements of safety training. By setting up experiences that may frighten the horse in a safe environment, we can work on habituating him to the things he will encounter in the wider world like plastic bags on fences or cars. In addition to habituating the horse, we can also train ourselves to give calm signals to him at the same time. If we concentrate on breathing and relaxing our bodies, the horse will understand that we don't think the situation is dangerous. I also like to teach an 'it's all right' cue, such as a light scratch on the withers that I can later use when out riding as a means of reassurance.

His Lifestyle

The first step to making a horse safe is to make him calm. An important factor in this is that he feels at peace with the world, and his living conditions are the key to this. If we consider how much time we actually spend with our horses, we may think we do quite well if we see them every day and ride them three times a week. But let's consider it from the other side. Most horses probably spend around 24 hours a day not in our company. Timewise, we are an insignificant part of their lives, despite the fact that they only exist because we want them to. If a horse can spend that large proportion of his life doing what he is designed to do by nature, this will mitigate many of the difficulties he may have with the time he spends with us.

Horses need to move as much as possible, to have constant access to forage and to have company. Therefore, we must keep them in a way that maximizes these three factors while providing adequate shelter, correct feed and good hoof care. Many people feel disadvantaged by the idea of allowing their horses a more natural lifestyle because so few livery yards are set up to allow it. However, there are small steps that can still be taken to provide a more ideal environment.

> A horse that is content with his
> life because he can carry out his
> natural behaviour will be calmer and
> safe to ride.

Suggestions for improving the livery environment

○ Make a pen outside the stable to increase the area the horse has to move.

○ Keep horses together in larger paddocks rather than separating them in small turnout plots, thus fulfilling their desire for companionship.

○ Open a space between loose boxes so that neighbours can mutually groom, allowing much closer friendships to form between horses.

○ Give a choice of forage (hay, unmolassed sugar beet, dried lucerne) and place it in different places in the stable, allowing the horse to carry out a more natural foraging behaviour.

○ If possible, simply open the stable door and give the horse the choice to come and go as he pleases. Horses will always use the full amount of space available to them, be that a yard or twenty acres; you never see a horse choosing to limit himself to an area twelve feet by twelve feet.

Education

The second step to having a safe horse lies in what the horse actually learns from us. This is distinct from what we think we are teaching. Frightening behaviour may arise because the horse is unfamiliar with something and therefore reacts with caution, seen by him raising himself a hand and snorting dramatically. It may be that he tries to move away from the object of his fear. Both reactions can be frightening to the handler because we don't know what the horse is going to do next. My reaction to a horse I know well is often one of amusement, but with a horse I don't know, I will be more cautious and will have a certain amount of adrenalin flowing whilst endeavouring to appear confident and without tension. Like ours, the horse's reactions are perfectly natural. They have evolved to be suspicious of any novelty and change in their environment and, compared to the plains where not much changes, the world of humans means variety. We must, therefore, train the horse to cope.

There is a tendency to believe that horses should simply know what we expect of them and this, of course, is impossible. Horses have to be taught what we want them to do and training is the process by which we accomplish this. They also have to be able to do what we ask them. Just because there are people who can do the splits doesn't mean that I am able to. Similarly, just because a horse is a horse doesn't mean he can necessarily do a counter canter and, just as I can see no earthly reason why I should do the splits, there is no reason to a horse why he should perform a counter canter. His performance comes down to good training.

Human error in training is one of the most common causes of horses being dangerous. If the horse doesn't understand what is required of him and is punished for his reaction, he will quickly decide to get out of the situation. Of course, he is prevented from doing so and some degree of panic often ensues. A horse that is regularly subjected to harsh, confusing training will end up in a state of flight-or-fight every time he is worked and will associate being ridden with danger.

To make yourself feel safer, establish a personal space around you that the horse can enter when invited.

Teaching the horse what is acceptable to you from the beginning is important in preventing dangerous behaviour developing. We accept some behaviour, such as nibbling, head rubbing and standing close because we are flattered by the attention the horse is giving us. But nibbling can develop into nipping, and head rubbing or standing too close give the horse the idea that we don't have a personal body space, which in turn may lead to head-butting and barging. It is helpful therefore, to establish clear limits when it comes to any behaviour that involves physical contact. Having a clearly defined personal boundary into which the horse only comes when invited is worthwhile and is something that horses understand clearly as it's a central feature of their interactions with one another. This works both ways: have respect for your horse's personal space and approach gently, and your horse will find you more pleasant to have around.

Having a choice

Many riders never truly get to choose their horse. Riding schools make an effort to pair horse and rider along the lines of size and experience, but if you are riding someone else's horse, or taking a horse on loan, you can't be too fussy. Even buying a horse is still limited by time, budgets and distance of travel. However, a lot of problems could be avoided if more care is taken in matching up horse and rider.

Helen's story   Helen was in her mid-thirties when she bought her first horse, a 15.2 skewbald schoolmaster called Pippin. He was safe in traffic, jumped, did cross country and dressage at riding-club level, and Helen had a wonderful time enjoying the freedom of owning a horse. Unfortunately, after two years he was diagnosed with navicular syndrome and was destroyed on the advice of a vet. Helen was heartbroken and began the search for another horse.

The people at her livery yard encouraged her to go for a more glamorous animal, something bigger and supposedly better bred, so after searching for a few weeks, she bought a sixteen-hand Cleveland Bay cross, called Max. Helen felt a little apprehensive about the horse. It was a struggle to mount him and he was rather wide, but to begin with, he behaved well when ridden in the school.

Helen really wanted to ride out and hoped to do pleasure rides with Max. The first ride was not a success, however. Max became highly excited, leaving Helen feeling out of control. She was demoralized by this experience but her husband encouraged her, pointing out that Max hadn't really had time to settle in and that they were still in the process of getting used to each other.

Helen tried to hack out regularly, allowing Max to sort himself out. They progressed to trotting and cantering, but then, just as she was feeling they were getting somewhere, Max bucked her off. She'd asked him to canter gently along a short grass track and suddenly she was on the ground with Max standing looking at her. Helen was shaken. She had no choice but to lead him home where the livery yard owner offered to ride him and he behaved perfectly. Nervously, Helen mounted, rode some circles and the horse continued to behave. Her confidence had been undermined by the fall but she persevered, hoping that the buck was a one-off.

Unfortunately, it wasn't. Max began to put in huge bucks for no apparent reason and on one occasion, one of his hooves hit Helen in the back of the head as she fell. An expert checked his back and saddle but nothing could be found that would account for his behaviour. It appeared that when he was getting to a point where he didn't want to do something, he would simply dispose of his rider. It wasn't just Helen who produced such behaviour; an instructor rode Max and the horse put on a spectacular display of rodeo bucking. Helen's husband stopped speaking up for him and wanted the horse sold before his wife ended up in hospital. Helen agreed as she had lost all desire to ride. They phoned Max's previous owner who, despite claiming he'd never bucked with her, took him back and returned their money.

Helen began the hunt for another horse, determined not to give up riding yet aware that it was going to take a lot to repair her confidence. She phoned a recommended dealer and explained she was looking for a sensible, and preferably coloured horse. Two weeks later she received a call from the dealer to say a load of horses had just arrived from Ireland and there was one she thought would be suitable for Helen.

Helen headed over to the yard feeling nervous. She hadn't ridden since Max had gone and was having doubts about whether she would ever ride again. The dealer was encouraging and led her to a loose box saying, 'I know you didn't want a horse with too much white on him, but I have something special…' The horse was a 14.3-hand, piebald cob, with rather more white than black. 'This is Piper,' explained the dealer. 'He's only four but he's so level-headed.'

Helen agreed to try the horse. With butterflies in her stomach, she mounted. Piper seemed unfazed by everything, which, considering he'd only arrived a couple of days before, impressed Helen. She felt confident enough to ride along a country road, her nerves vanishing as she began to enjoy being in the saddle again. Then she heard a loud engine, and a tractor, with its amber light flashing, appeared round the corner towards them. Trying to breathe deeply but panicking inside, Helen asked Piper to step into a gateway, which he did. She watched his reaction. He hardly flicked an ear and stood calmly as the tractor crawled by, the driver waving cheerily. Helen didn't dare take a hand off the reins to return the gesture, but Piper, as if wondering what the fuss was about, rested one back leg and began to investigate the verge for a snack. That was it. He had sold himself.

Since then, Helen and Piper have done thousands of miles of riding, completing a coast-to-coast ride and a long-distance cross-country trek. They have taken part in a range of riding-club disciplines and been in numerous endurance rides. The dealer's description of Piper as level headed was accurate; he's one of those equines that doesn't fulfil the stereotype of the horse as a flight animal, but stops and thinks about what to do in any situation. Helen does have one complaint about him though: when it comes to brushing the mud off, he still has too much white!

The right type

When choosing a horse, just like choosing a partner, it is important to separate our romantic dreams from reality. The dream horse and what we can do together have to be tempered by two variables: the horse itself, and ourselves. Surprisingly, this second factor is the starting point. Let me take myself as an example. I'm 5ft 3in and of medium weight. I have a slightly stiff right hip, so I don't want a horse that's too wide. I'm an experienced rider and enjoy riding young horses, and horses with certain behavioural 'issues'; but thanks to my first pony, I'm not confident about jumping and I have no desire to do dressage. I'm happiest riding over the moors on an enthusiastic horse, small enough to open gates from, go under low branches and be mounted from the ground. If we take each of my characteristics and match them to a suitable horse, he comes out as being 14-handish, forward going, age immaterial, reasonably stocky, and perhaps with a few behavioural issues to work on. Therefore, I won't go and buy a 16-hand warmblood that comes from a long line of eventers.

However, if I had a vision of myself in white jodhpurs and shiny leather boots on a glistening horse and winning dressage tests, I might be inclined to go for that 16-hand warmblood despite the reality of myself as a rider. I'm not saying we should all go for safe, stocky cobs but to get to the white jodhpur stage, I may have to do a lot of work on myself before buying the dressage horse. That horse can no more make me a dressage rider than I can make my stocky cob a Grand Prix dressage horse. I may need to start with a mount on which I can learn to ride well enough before progressing to the dressage horse, and I would definitely need to give my cob to an experienced trainer to teach him to do dressage. And there would certainly be no point in having that dressage horse if I was too scared to get on it!

This is not to say that the horse world is divided into big, posh dangerous horses and scruff, little safe ones, as many bruised children can testify. Assessing the character of an individual equine is essential when choosing your horse. It's easy to fall into the trap of labelling certain breeds and types as having certain personality characteristics, even though this is true to some

> When choosing a horse, we need to be
> realistic about ourselves as riders
> and the animal we are aiming for.

extent. If we have selectively bred for desirable physical characteristics, we have probably done the same for personality, usually inadvertently. But caution needs to be taken when looking at personality and breeding. It is simple to say that Thoroughbreds tend to be highly strung and coloured cobs sensible, but there are not many Thoroughbreds that have been raised by the side of a road, and probably no coloured cobs that have come through the racing system. It's the old 'nature versus nurture' debate.

Our expectations of breeds frequently lead us to approach them in a certain way. Fell and Dales ponies are an interesting example. With a reputation for being bolshie and often bred by hill men, there is an attitude that they have to be trained in a heavy-handed manner. However, in my experience, Fells and Dales are amongst the most sensitive of horses but their reputation arises from the fact that they tend to shut down when frightened – much like donkeys. Hence they are labelled stubborn and strong-willed. When handled lightly, though, they are as soft and responsive as the most highly bred, hot-blooded horse, and the moments when they do say 'no' can usually be dealt with by firm insistence and good humour, with the occasional resort to outwitting them using superior human brainpower. In a herd of mixed types and breeds, all kept and handled in the same way, it becomes harder to see personality as attached to breed and easier to see personality as individual.

Just as with humans, some horses are born level-headed, some require work to become calm, and some will always have a streak of flightiness. We are often tricked into thinking that buying a young horse is a good idea because horse and rider can learn together. In reality, the rider really needs to know what's going on because when that young horse asks a question, she needs to be able to give a correct answer. If you are the one asking the questions, you need a horse that can give the answers. Age does not necessarily bring wisdom, however; not all horses progress to being sensible schoolmasters and we can all name animals that are as spirited at twenty as they were at four. Similarly, if you do find a calm, sensible four-year-old that feels right, then don't be put off by his age, but do be aware that he will still need to be treated as 'green' because there may be something somewhere that will be outside his experience. The past history of the horse is also important. An ex-racehorse may seem like a bargain, but needs a particular approach and re-training.

Size is important

The relationship between size and weight-carrying capacity of the horse is more complicated than it may initially sound.

There is a tendency to think that the bigger the rider, the taller the horse should be but, in fact, weight-carrying has less to do with the height at the wither than the strength through the loins, the area where the back joins the rump. A short-coupled horse will find it easier to carry weight than a long-backed horse, and even horses that have a leg at each corner may still be weak in the loin area. Incidentally, there is evidence to suggest that however big and strong the horse, the weight of a rider of more than 95 kilograms or 15 stone cannot be adequately dissipated by any saddle so sore areas on the back will be caused by the resultant pressure.

It is a characteristic of the United Kingdom that we ride big horses. In the USA and Australia, 15 hands is considered a good size for a man to ride, and the fact that the rider's feet may hang below the horse's belly is of no consequence. Once horses get beyond a certain size, they have more problems breathing, keeping cool and staying sound, so perhaps we'd be doing them a favour if we started breeding for smaller, stronger horses.

A small rider will find a large horse less manageable than a smaller one, but again the issue is not simply one of height. Short legs may mean that a narrow 15-hand horse will enable you to achieve a secure seat that would be impossible on a wide 14-hand pony that took up most of your leg length in a horizontal direction. When choosing a horse, we need to look at our own conformation and physical limitations as well as those of the horse.

> Choose a horse that is comfortable
> for you to both ride and handle.

What sex? What colour?

The sex of the horse is often of great importance to people although I have never found there to be a problem with mares being difficult or geldings being unresponsive. There is as much variation within the individuals of any group of mares or geldings (or stallions for that matter) as there is between the two groups, and despite the current trend today, mares and geldings can be kept together and seem to enjoy each other's company.

There is also a strong inclination to want a horse of a certain colour or not. Again, although a grey may require more keeping clean, I haven't found any real difference between colours, despite the reputation of chestnuts for being fiery. With regard to character, it may be another case of seeing what we expect to see, as with the breeds and sexes. Thirty years ago coloured horses were frowned on, yet today you can get almost any type with patches. Had I been fussy about greys or chestnuts, mares or geldings, I would have missed knowing some of the wonderful horses I've had. As the cowboy saying goes, a good horse is never a bad colour.

Trying the horse

Assessing a horse means seeing how he reacts in a variety of situations, and particularly the one you are planning for in the long term. As the story of Helen and Piper demonstrates, had Helen only tried the horse in the school, she would never have had the opportunity to see how he reacted to the tractor on the road. Observe how the horse behaves; notice whether he is quiet in the field or stable, for example. Care needs to be taken not to confuse a horse that has shut down or is depressed with a truly calm one, though. A horse should be interested in his surroundings, the people who visit and other horses; one that has given up and tolerates everything has learned that displaying displeasure does not get him results, and often invites punishment. Such a horse is likely to feel some release of pressure when he is moved to a more acceptable environment and a whole range of behaviour you don't want may emerge, although usually a sense of relief and relaxation will be seen. The characteristics we are looking for are a kind, relaxed eye, interest and willingness to cooperate. Take a moment to stand quietly with the horse and see if he sniffs you all over and wants to make contact. This would be a promising introduction.

It is sensible to watch the horse being handled and ridden before you do anything with him. The old advice was always to see him being caught in the field, attended to in the stable, groomed and tacked up. I like to go further by spending time watching him at liberty and just being with him. In this way, I can get an initial feel for the animal. After all, if this is going to be my mount for the foreseeable future, I want to make sure I actually like him and he seems all right about me. He may be the tenth one I've looked at and may fit the bill for height, price, age and ability, but if I don't feel comfortable about him, he isn't the right horse for me.

A good tip is not only to watch the horse, but to watch the handler as well, as this gives an indication of how the animal has been treated and may explain the behaviour you see. For example, if the horse scowls and blows out when girthed up, notice whether this is because the girth is hauled up tightly as soon as the saddle is put on his back. It doesn't mean that the horse is a bad character or doesn't like being ridden, simply that he finds rough girthing uncomfortable.

It is important to see the horse actually doing what you want to do with him. This may sound obvious, but it's common to buy a horse having only ridden him in circles in a school when what you actually want to do is hack out. If you want to jump in future, even if you aren't confident enough to do it yet, get the seller to put the horse over a small obstacle. Don't fall for the demonstration where the horse is placed on the lunge and chased over a

> When buying a horse, try to see him
> doing what you plan to do with him.

huge jump to show that he has a 'pop' in him. If your aim is to achieve a
clear round at the riding club by the end of next year, it's not the size of the
spread that matters to you; all you want to see is that the horse is
comfortable and willing to jump, not that he's a puissance prospect!

Getting to know your horse

As a child, I was amazed by a book I read
called *Wish for a Pony.* When the girl in the story finally
got her first pony, he was delivered to her house but she didn't ride him
straightaway. I was sure that when eventually I got that longed-for pony, I
would be on his back and off over the hills as the last hoof left the ramp.
Some years later, when my first pony arrived, I'm glad to say I didn't leap into
the saddle and gallop off, but spent some time getting to know him first.

If you are not completely confident about riding, there is nothing wrong
with getting to know your horse from the ground to begin with. In fact, this
is good practice and does not only apply to a horse you've bought; if you are
exercising a friend's horse or even riding at a riding school, you may be able
to organize extra time to spend with the horse before getting on board.
Grooming him, going for walks, hanging around in the field and watching is
all good preparation.

From the horse's point of view, not being ridden immediately may be a
relief as changing home is a huge disruption. In feral horse groups, one of
the rare situations that leads to aggression is when a new horse comes into
the herd, the disruption of changing location and companions being highly
unsettling. In our domestic situation, the following scenarios are typical
when a horse acquires a new owner and environment. The first is that there
is a honeymoon period when everything goes smoothly, then after a time,
things begin to unravel and fall apart. In the second, the horse immediately

attempts to see what he can 'get away with', transmuting from the perfect animal you agreed to buy into an unpredictable hooligan. Both of these can be explained in part by the fact that the horse has had his whole life changed and is in a situation with new rules and routines. Giving him a few weeks to settle in is a good strategy anyway, and more so if you are not completely confident in the saddle. You can work out each other's ground rules and build up some trust without the worry of riding. This means that you can be clear about your expectations in safe situations; for example, that you won't allow the horse to tow you when leading, or you will insist on him stepping back when you enter the stable. This is important because some horses have learned that certain humans can be pushed around and not taken seriously, so clear indications of what you will and won't accept will establish the balance of your relationship.

A settling-in period also gives you time to learn how your horse reacts to things around him and what bothers him, so that when you come to ride, you will have more idea of what to expect and may even be able to avoid potentially dangerous situations. Your new horse will appreciate having one less thing to worry about, too. After all, he'll probably be dealing with a new set of friends who are of far more concern to him than what you want him to do.

The riding instructor

If you lack confidence or are learning to ride, it is really vital that you find a sympathetic instructor who understands what you are comfortable with. Learning to ride should essentially be a blame-free process. There is no point blaming the horse for not doing what you want, and similarly, there is no point being blamed yourself. There is even less point blaming bits of your body, so having 'Heels down!' yelled at you will be of no help at all. Riding is about moving without tension, so a sergeant-major-like manner in an instructor will be inappropriate. You may find that working on your own body away from the horse, through activities such as yoga, the Alexander Technique, the

Finding a sympathetic instructor
will help you to increase your
confidence with your horse.

Feldenkrais method or with a physical therapist will make a great difference when you are in the saddle.

If an instructor suggests anything that you feel unhappy about, you have every right to refuse to do it. For example, I know of one who lunged a horse for forty minutes on the left rein because the animal was stiff on that side, yet the owner felt unable to say she thought this was wrong, if not actually cruel. The expertise of the instructor goes so far, but let common sense and intuition guide you, too.

How to make the most of your riding lesson

○ Be clear what you want from your instructor.

○ Talk to the instructor first to find out more about his or her approach.

○ Try to watch a lesson to see if you like the style.

○ Explain in advance what frightens you.

○ During the lesson don't be pushed into anything that scares you.

What we can expect from horses

Hopefully we've established that, if they are treated properly, horses aren't out to get us, and they're not dangerous animals we need to fear. It's worth considering the more subconscious fears we may have about them, however; those associated with our perception of their feelings towards us.

All people who interact with horses do so because horses meet certain needs and desires, and within this, the amount of emotional involvement varies. At one end of the spectrum is the desire to make money, with the horse as a commodity. Generally, racehorse owners don't tend to have deep emotional attachments to their horses simply for the reason that they love the personality of a particular horse. The basic desire is to compete, win and make money. Similarly, many people who compete at all levels are willing to buy and sell horses depending on their success in competition. Jumping ponies get passed from home to home as the child moves out of each height category. Of course, people do become attached to some individual characters, as can be seen when the old 'first pony' remains at the racing yard, seeing scores of Thoroughbreds pass through.

At the other end of the spectrum the horse becomes the focus for deeper emotional feelings. Consider the number of horses that are kept in this country but barely ridden. For many, owning a horse is the fulfilment of a childhood dream and, as mentioned earlier, that dream is often of the romantic fiction variety and doesn't have a lot to do with the reality of horse ownership. Some horses are kept because the owner simply enjoys caring for another living being. Cleaning the stable, buying a new rug, washing and grooming, buying food supplements, worrying about health, all fill a basic need in such a person. For many of us, spending time with a horse is an escape from the demands of family and work. It is our time away from constantly having to answer to other people.

> Try to spend some time with your
> horse that doesn't involve you making
> demands on him.

Our needs versus the horse's needs

The choice of how we spend our time with the horse is important and varies in value in terms of building a confident and safe relationship with him. Mucking out, changing rugs and sweeping up aren't going to help because they are catering to needs that we have invented for the horse – living in a stable, needing clothing and keeping the place tidy, respectively. Given food, space, water, shelter and company, a horse will look after himself, with minimal intervention from us and will benefit from the freedom, both mentally and physically. To improve relations, we must spend time in ways the horse appreciates. The crux of this human behaviour is that a lot of emotions are invested in the horse that, frankly, he does not have the faintest need or understanding of. But we humans expect something back. We want our horses to love us. We look for the signs that they like us, recognize us, and look forward to our arrival. We worry that maybe our horses don't love us or even like us and this is another source of fear.

Horses, however, don't operate like that. Certainly their social bonds with one another are strong; they mutually groom and stay close to each other, they hate to be alone and, in some cases, when separated will act as though bereft. But at the same time, at any given moment, they will ignore each other, move away or be actively hostile even to a close friend. They don't take offence about this; they simply do not mind if another horse doesn't want to communicate with them that day. We humans, however, do, and so we become afraid that our horses don't feel towards us as we feel towards them.

Understanding our relationship with the horse

How do we overcome this fear of not being loved?

First, we need to accept that we are never going to become our horse's significant 'other', and if we did, the relationship would be abnormal and possibly detrimental to the horse. There are some animals that have been so over-trained and institutionalized that they can't cope without a particular human, but horses should be friends with other horses. There is no way I can expect the degree of friendship from my horse that he has with his field mates. I have no right to because I spend, at best, two or three hours a day some days of the week in his company. Once we accept this, we can lose the fear about horses not loving us.

Secondly, we have to recognize how horses actually show interest in us, and to do this we have to get rid of the 'tool' that produces false interest, titbits. It's easy to get a horse's attention with food and it's nice to think that the nicker in the morning is because he's glad to see you, or the enthusiasm to nuzzle your hand is about affection, when actually you are simply being viewed as a vending machine.

The real compliment your horse can pay you is when he approaches you purely to say hello. His acknowledgement may take the form of a look towards you with pricked ears, it may be an approach, you may even be lucky enough that he follows you of his own will, but these are the subtleties of a horse's emotional expression towards others. 'I went to visit my old horse and he didn't even recognize me,' is a lament I often hear and the response is always the same: don't expect a horse to jump up and down wagging his tail when he sees you. If you want that reaction, it would be better to buy a dog! It's highly probable that he did recognize you, but that's not how horses express themselves. The more they recognize you, the less interesting you are to them. So, if we learn to accept the way horses offer affection, we can take as much delight and fulfilment from receiving it as we get from the idiotic joy of a dog on our appearance, or of a child choosing to talk to us.

Constantly doing things to a horse in an attempt to get him to like you will probably have the opposite effect as animals often gravitate to the calm person

Treat your horse with respect and
compassion for his nature as a horse.

not paying them too much attention; witness the cat choosing to sit on the knee of the person who doesn't particularly like cats. If you are comfortable to be with, your horse is more likely to want to be with you.

None of this is to say that you shouldn't love your horse or use your relationship with him to fulfil an emotional need; just don't do it to the detriment of his life. When it comes down to it, a horse is a horse, and needs to be respected as such. He is unlikely to accompany you into a peaceful old age: in fact, the sad reality is that you are likely to be the one who makes the decision about when to end his old age, something that must be done with only the horse's interest at heart. The responsibility of having to decide when it is right to end a life is the most difficult one we take on. To do right by the horse, we have to approach it with compassion, not sentimentality.

It doesn't have to be riding

What do you do if, after every effort, you still find riding to be a frightening experience and yet you are perfectly happy to be around horses on the ground? It may be that you already have a horse you cannot bear to part with and yet riding him is simply not an option. Perhaps you have always loved horses and have learned to understand them but have no desire to venture on to their backs. Are there any alternatives to keeping or being around horses, and not riding them?

It is perfectly acceptable to admit that you are frightened of something and choose not to do it. I don't do anything that involves being underwater, for example. I don't snorkel, scuba dive, canoe or even dive off the side of a pool. But I do swim and enjoy going in the sea. Choosing not to ride doesn't mean not owning a horse; there are many horses that need a home that can't be ridden due to age or injury. Think about the pleasure you can get from simply having the horse there, grooming him, taking him for walks, perhaps teaching him tricks to keep him from boredom, or just watching him. The social interactions of horses are fascinating and will probably teach you more about them than any number of hours in the saddle. This also gives you the option of having a horse or pony that may be less intimidating in terms of size and cheaper to keep.

If you still don't feel comfortable handling horses, even on the ground, but your love for them is still a motivating factor, there are other ways you can be involved with them. You could volunteer to help with an organization such as Riding for the Disabled or at a horse rescue centre; you could sponsor a pony from such a centre under a scheme that allows you to contribute to his upkeep and visit him, but leaves the handling to others. You could get involved at your local riding club or with an agricultural show as an usher or organizer. If you have a good equestrian knowledge, you may even be able to judge.

A final thought

Being afraid of horses is an understandable and, at times, appropriate reaction.

However, a lot of the fear we feel can be overcome. By understanding the nature of the horse, learning to read the language they use and becoming more comfortable with them, it is possible to enjoy the pleasure of riding and handling horses. If you have lost confidence, the first step is to find out what you feel comfortable with and to work within those limits. With time, you may well find your confidence increasing and decide it's time to get back in the saddle – and even if you don't, it's likely that you can still find a way to enjoy horses.

3
Teaching the Nervous Rider

Christina Barlow

'The only effective, long-term solution to fear relating to horses and to riding them is the regular and consistent implementation of practical and workable exercises, behaviours and riding habits, calculated specifically to ensure that we do in fact become safer and more confident around horses.'

Understanding fear

Fear transcends all horse-riding disciplines and all levels of equestrian expertise.

Some people experience fear from the outset of their contact with horses; for others it occurs suddenly after years of mostly uneventful riding. For many it is the predictable result of an accident that affected them most profoundly, leaving them with a persistent and convincing sense of foreboding. But in a large number of cases the fear is without an apparent cause, consisting only of a general dread of getting hurt somehow.

In some cases, the fear can become so debilitating that the beginner gives up riding altogether or the experienced rider stops competing, often without revealing to anyone the extent of their fears. In many other cases, the rider perseveres, often silently, while trying to suppress the fear just far enough to continue riding, albeit without deriving much pleasure from it.

The main reasons that so many fearful riders never make any meaningful effort to seek help are because they are too embarrassed to admit it to others, and because they can deduce from the general behaviour and remarks of some people that 'being afraid of horses' is seen as a weakness. At many riding establishments the subject of fear is virtually taboo. At others it is treated with a dismissive attitude, bordering on sneering contempt for anyone daring to admit to it or appearing to be suffering from it.

This culture of 'false fearlessness' around horses leaves many a rider feeling like a complete failure whenever they suffer a lapse in confidence, and it could even be partly responsible for feeding a sense of fear amongst novice riders by enforcing the erroneous belief in many of them that they and they alone suffer from it. The truth is that even the most experienced and so-called 'fearless' riders probably do succumb to occasional bouts of fear as well. They have just had years of practice at hiding it well enough to continue competing and instructing. Indeed, one often hears a rider claiming to have had a 'great ride' after having witnessed that same person being involved in an enormous power struggle with her horse to get it to respond to cues (aids) or to willingly submit to attempts at control. In cases such as these the

It is natural to feel apprehension as to whether we can control an animal so much more powerful than ourselves.

rider apparently feels obliged to say they have enjoyed the experience, regardless of whether it was any fun at all.

Many riders caught in this 'ride-or-be-damned' trap have been around horses for a long time but simply know no other way of doing things. Some would even be taken aback at the mere suggestion that fear was something worthy of dedicated attention, and certainly would not merit it, a topic for lengthy discussion.

Despite this large-scale denial of the existence of such fear, responsible horse-riding instructors know that it is actually perfectly natural for human beings to feel apprehensive regarding their ability to control an animal that is so much bigger and more powerful than themselves. These instructors also accept that a fear of horses or horse riding can be brought about by a multitude of external causes, including thoughtless riding instruction, that give complete validity to the emotion.

The causes of fear

The fear of horses or riding can occur for many reasons. The most common causes include:

- A deeply frightening experience like a horse bolting, bucking or rearing
- A disturbing encounter with a horse on the ground, such as being bitten, kicked or intimidated by an animal that is disrespectful to humans
- A fall or near-fall, whether the rider suffers injury or not
- A mismatch between horse and rider

- Buying or riding a horse with established and/or dangerous vices
- Witnessing another rider being involved in an accident
- Becoming intimidated by 'horror' stories told by other riders about a particular horse or riding incident
- Feeling under pressure to fulfil the expectations of parents, peers or an instructor
- Feeling inferior in the company of very competent or overconfident riders
- The normal apprehension felt by novices, especially adults, who begin riding late in life
- Acts of nature scaring a horse, for example, wind or lightning
- An unsympathetic instructor.

Novice and competent riders alike can be taken completely by surprise when a horse suddenly does something that puts the rider at physical risk. This could simply be the result of the horse spooking at a gust of wind or a loud noise and could occur on the ground as easily as when the rider is mounted. If she were injured in such an incident, it would be almost unnatural or superhuman not to develop concerns for her future well-being around horses.

Injuries do not have to be physical, of course. While many falls off a horse's back leave the rider with nothing more bruised than their ego, many others retain a more or less recurring image of the event in their minds. This leaves them vulnerable to persistent worry that can easily turn into full-blown fear. Similarly, seeing a horse and rider involved in an accident often impacts powerfully on the subconscious of the witness, leaving many people with the niggling fear that it could happen to them, too.

Inexperienced riders and first-time horse buyers often over-horse themselves by trying to ride a particular horse or by buying one that is too spirited for them at the time. The result can be an unfortunate incident, even a complete and terrifying loss of control, which might not have happened on a more submissive animal. Understandably, that rider may develop a deep fear of the event recurring even when mounted on a quieter horse in future. Living up to the ideals of horse-riding glory that others may hold for them

Behind the creation of fear is often a
vice-ridden horse, a pushy parent or
an unsympathetic instructor.

can put many a rider in an impossible situation of trying to perform faultlessly and fearlessly on cue. This pressure alone is enough to make some people become fearful, if only of being able to ride a particular horse in a particular manner at all times.

Behind the creation or the re-creation of fear is often a horse with a potentially perilous vice. Whether the rider has created the vice through ignorance or arrogance, or whether she has chosen a horse with a vice because she has overestimated her capabilities, or after being misled by a horse trader, such an animal is almost guaranteed to provide experiences that will instil acute fear.

While fear is less common in younger riders, many adults and elderly people, who are more aware of their own physical fragility, do feel deeply nervous, especially if they are complete novices or have returned to riding after a long break.

case study

A fearful return My first ever student was Elizabeth, a former photojournalist with a phobia of handling and riding horses. A few months earlier she had returned to riding after an absence of nearly three decades spent on an all-consuming career. Her fears were rooted firmly in unpalatable memories of a childhood riding history of expensive, but unsuitably dangerous horses, and some very nasty accidents indeed. Like her father, her husband also dabbled in breeding and racing. Like her father, her husband had little patience with her 'affliction'. Trail rides with him often ended with him declaring, 'It's no fun riding with you. Let's turn back to the stable.' She had also had a quick succession of snooty riding instructors appointed by her husband who displayed only marginally more patience with nervous riders.

When Elizabeth approached me, she said that whenever she went near a horse, or even thought of riding, she became overwhelmed with feelings of foreboding, dread and disaster. In my opinion, only her inbred stoicism had prevented her from giving up horse riding completely and her fears could certainly not be brushed aside. However, by gently taking her back to basics and with patient and empathetic instruction, it was possible for her to completely rebuild her trust in horses, and to create a belief that she was indeed capable of handling and riding them in as safe a manner as possible. Admittedly it took several months, with the odd relapse in between, for Elizabeth to master the calm, consistent horse-handling skills she so needed, but today she is no longer afraid of horses. Instead, she has gained enormous respect for their power and has become a very vocal advocate of responsible horsemanship. Several years later, she still conscientiously practises the simple horse-handling and riding exercises that helped her overcome her fears, and uses those self-same skills to help other nervous riders of her acquaintance.

Many novices and instinctively nervous riders have seen their dreams of horseback joy diminished considerably by instructors who scorn fear to the point of irritability and impatience with students. Even some top instructors, who are brilliant at teaching the technical aspects of riding, expect their students to refrain from 'whining' and to 'just get on with it'. Many appear to have no real interest in dealing with the fears of their students, but seem intent only on ensuring that the dictates of a particular discipline are followed with relentless rigidity.

This style of instruction could leave such students feeling hopelessly inadequate because they are often too preoccupied with physical and mental survival to be able to absorb a significant amount of teaching, and too unsure of their horsemanship skills to ride with the required firmness and consistency. In time, a student in such a situation could develop a more or less permanent terror of both riding and instruction. It is therefore imperative for instructors to have a thorough understanding of the origins of fear and an acceptance and tolerance of its existence. Furthermore, the instructor has to translate that awareness of fear and its consequences into compassionate teaching traits that will build confidence instead of instilling or aggravating fear in a student.

> Cultivate a style of instruction
> calculated to build confidence instead
> of aggravating fear in a student.

Skills for teaching the nervous rider

In helping the nervous rider to overcome her fears, it is essential that instructors develop a number of vital teaching qualities.

O **Empathy in feeling.**

Avoid showing exasperation when teaching novices and those riders suffering from a temporary loss of confidence, as it is likely to worsen and entrench the anxiety rather than bring it to a conveniently quick dissolution. If you don't have the temperament and patience to deal with such riders, don't accept them as students.

O **Thoughtfulness in speech.**

Ghastly as this may sound, psychological bullying of students does seem to happen with astonishing frequency, especially in some disciplines. While confident and more advanced riders may cope with an abrasive style of instruction, it has exactly the opposite effect on a jittery student. This distinctly unhelpful mode of teaching also adds humiliation and shame to the student's bag of feelings.

O **Mindfulness of teaching style.**

Teaching habits that do not aid in building confidence include an air of distraction, an apparent lack of focus on the student and excessive clock watching. Those that an apprehensive student is most likely to benefit from include professional attention to her riding needs, patience in explaining instructions and aids, helpful advice during periods of frustration, sympathy in moments of distress, and honest comments on her progress.

O Responsibility in actions.

Do not act in ways that unnerve your student, either in your handling of horses or in your instruction of riders. Remember that the nervous student really does need to be around somebody whose calm handling of horses will make her feel that she has a chance of learning how to manage her own fears.

O Discretion in demeanour.

Few people would feel comfortable knowing that every rider at a particular stable yard, and even the occasional visitor, is kept fully informed of their pitiful experiences with horses. For most, the embarrassment factor would simply be too high. The majority of students are not likely to make significant progress in overcoming their fear of riding if they suspect that the instructor is laughing behind their backs. Some might even decide to seek refuge at another establishment.

hold the thought

Consistent, calm horse handling by the instructor gives the fearful student hope of mastering her own fears.

Dealing with nervous riders

Many nervous riders feel intimidated not only by the horses they have to ride, but also by other riders, many of who seem so much more able, confident and in control than themselves. If those riders also find themselves in an unsympathetic, or even hostile environment, it can become very difficult for them to overcome a fear of horses and of riding. That is why it is vitally important for everybody involved in equine instruction to ensure that their actions are not so bereft of understanding and compassion that they alienate novices or nervous riders from wanting to be with horses altogether.

This is particularly relevant for the riding instructor because it is often her sensitivity in dealing with the situation that could ultimately determine whether a rider will learn to manage fear or not. If the instructor is to succeed in this challenge, she not only has to develop compassionate teaching traits, but also has to observe certain guidelines in her work with the novice and nervous student.

The following guidelines are amongst the most important.

○ Remember: everybody in the equine industry started off knowing nothing about horses.
No one can be expected to have an innate knowledge of how to handle or ride horses confidently, and yet it is quite common, once one has become an accomplished rider, to forget that all of us had to start learning riding skills from scratch and that many of us also suffered from similar, if not worse, fears at one or more stages of our riding lives.

Such a thoughtless attitude on the part of an instructor can intensify, rather than alleviate, feelings of physical insecurity and other concerns a student has about her ability and future as a horse rider. To inspire the student, share with her your personal experiences of learning to manage fear.

○ **Don't foster a culture in which fear is something that is not talked about.**

Rather, actively encourage students to discuss their fears openly with you, while assuring them of your discretion. An invitation, sincerely issued, to a student to talk about her worst horse-related nightmares, should obviate the need for her to be full of fake bravado. It should also serve to lessen her potential embarrassment at having to bring it up, and should give the instructor a useful starting point for that student's lesson structures.

○ **Establish the exact nature of the student's fears as they relate to horses.**

Some people simply have a general fear of horses and/or riding, while others have a very specific concern. In this respect it is helpful to know on what exactly a student's fear is centred, so that fear in particular can be given priority treatment in her rehabilitation programme. Once a particular fear has been overcome, the student usually displays a marked increase in confidence. This makes it much easier to deal with any generalized fears still remaining.

○ **If possible find out the actual root cause of such a fear or fears.**

Once the particular fear has been identified, determine whether it came into existence as the result of an actual incident in which the student was injured or whether it exists because of something she imagined or heard could happen to her.

If a student's worries are born from personal experience, ask her to relate the event in detail to enable you to determine whether the accident occurred because of something done unintentionally by the rider, or whether it was caused by outside influences. If, for instance, a horse bucked with the rider because she had spurred it too closely to the flank, the first remedial step would be to help her practise the correct and safe positioning of legs, feet and heels when executing the aids, with special attention being paid to the amount of pressure applied when giving cues to the horse.

> The physical security of students always takes precedence over anything else the instructor may wish to teach.

If the accident happened because of non-rider-inspired behaviour on the part of the horse, the rider should be introduced to appropriate groundwork exercises and taught how to use these to predetect the possibility of a recurrence of such behaviour in that particular horse, or of it happening in any other horse that she may have to ride in the future.

O **Don't dismiss any fears as unfounded or as invalid.**

Just because we don't share another rider's fears or don't see the same dangers they perceive does not make their feelings, or the perils in them, any less real.

Fobbing off nervous riders with statements like, 'Oh don't worry, that won't happen …' or, 'That can never happen …' is not only an insult to the student's intelligence but also amounts to irresponsibility on the part of the instructor, who could not possibly, under any circumstances whatsoever, guarantee the safety of a student.

Downplaying any possible dangers related to horses and riding, and behaving defiantly as if accidents can't or won't happen, may give some students an entirely false sense of security that could endanger their lives at a later stage. Should the rider have an accident despite the instructor's assurances to the contrary, she will most certainly lose trust in the instructor and also in her judgement and professionalism.

It is the unquestionable duty of any instructor to ensure that the physical security of students always takes precedence over anything else she may wish to teach or achieve, and that safety rules are practised routinely, and regardless of how confident a rider becomes.

○ **Don't make students feel silly or embarrassed about their fears.**

If a novice or nervous rider has to suffer potentially humiliating remarks from an instructor who 'doesn't believe in babying riders', it could add significantly to her discomfort around horses. Even so-called 'harmless teasing' can increase a student's nervous apprehension, diminish her confidence and affect her willingness, and ability, to overcome her fears.

○ **Help students to regard their fears as a positive starting point from which to become responsible horsemen, not a disability.**

One doesn't have to congratulate a student on her fear, but often the first positive step in helping her to deal with it is to point out the possibilities inherent in an emotion she perceives to be entirely negative. If she can be persuaded to believe in the 'usefulness' of fear in eventually creating respect in herself for horses, then she is ready to be introduced to steps to do so. Many students who have succeeded in using their fear as a tool of transformation and improvement are eventually able to look back on its initial existence as a blessing.

○ **Make students aware of how those positive qualities they already possess could prevent their worst fears from being realized.**

Virtually every aspirant rider, whether a novice or a nerve-wracked old-timer who has had too many falls, has at least one quality that could help her become a good horsewoman. The instructor should try to discover any existing relevant quality as quickly as possible and use it as a tool of encouragement to the rider.

Some students will, for instance, exhibit a natural balance in the saddle while others may display instinctively light hands. By picking up on this and pointing out its possible benefits, the instructor will give the student an early and usually much needed boost of confidence. By regularly reminding the student of an ability that is either inherent or already

> Transform the student's fear into
> respect by teaching practical skills
> that will tangibly build confidence.

mastered, she is more likely to persevere in attaining the other qualities necessary to become a more confident rider.

O **Don't ignore the fears of a student in the hope that they will go away by themselves.**
An instructor's insistence on ignoring fear in a student will certainly not negate its continued existence, nor is it likely to shorten its duration or severity. Not only is it difficult for students to ingest and retain technical instruction while their attention is diverted by a fear which has not yet been dealt with, it is equally difficult for the horse to respond correctly to a fearful rider who is apt to give it confusing messages. Most riders really do need to take concrete, visible steps to overcome their fears, if they wish to do so in any meaningful and lasting way.

O **Don't try and 'order' the fear away.**
Some instructors deal with a student's fears in the way that is easiest for them as instructors, just commanding, 'Don't worry!'. Perhaps it is human perversity, but many people who are told not to worry tend to worry even more, especially if the platitude is uttered seemingly without much conviction or without any believable reason being given as to why it should not be necessary to do so.

Being repeatedly told to 'relax' doesn't help much either. It is not really possible to command another person to change their feelings without also presenting them with just cause and the means to do so. The student will only be able to relax once she actually feels in control of the horse.

O Teach the student practical ways in which to manage a particular fear as soon as you become aware of it, and don't withhold any relevant information.

It is vitally important for a student's safety that she knows as many different practical ways as possible to prevent or manage threatening situations. Furthermore, it is never appropriate to be mean with information at our disposal, or to give advice from which an important detail is missing.

O Be alert to serious emotional problems in a student.

No instructor should be expected to indulge riders whose fears are not really horse-related at all but could be the manifestation of other psychological problems requiring specialized treatment. This obviously does not pertain to students who just feel sad about something in particular or who are going through a temporary rough patch at home or at work, or to any of the normal emotional see-sawing of human beings, but to riders whose behaviour indicates persistent psychological trouble. Such cases, which a perceptive instructor should be able to pick up on quite quickly, are not likely to be cured completely by any amount of understanding or instruction.

For the sake of the instructor's peace of mind and professional survival, and the future mental health of the rider, it would be wise if the student could be diplomatically discouraged from relying on the lessons, the instructor or the horse for emotional survival. In certain extreme cases, where the rider, for instance, shows an unhealthy dependence on the instructor, lessons may have to be suspended or terminated.

> Serious psychological problems in a
> student cannot be cured by horses or a
> riding instructor alone.

case study

An unhealthy dependency... Edward, a social worker, believed that good horsemanship meant being able to race his friends on horseback and not fall off. His relief on being told that this kind of 'gung-ho' behaviour was the very antithesis of responsible riding was touching and I looked forward to helping him build confidence around horses. During the first few sessions, Edward remained determinedly nervous; his demeanour would vary from mere jumpiness around the horses to utter panic when a horse as much as picked up speed – even when I was leading it.

However, he did appear to comprehend the chain of fear that could develop between a rider and a horse, and how the rider could actually rob a horse of its confidence by fearful handling. Over time, his nervousness genuinely seemed to abate and eventually all our sessions were conducted with him remaining completely calm and in control of himself and the horse.

I was pleased with him and for him, and suggested that he was ready for more advanced lessons with another instructor. At once, all the symptoms of his previous fears returned. I was completely baffled at this and didn't succeed in obtaining a coherent explanation from him either. Undaunted, I started all over again with him. But things played out the same way again. And again. Every time I concluded that his confidence level was high enough for him not to need my help any more, he would have a relapse, sometimes quite dramatically.

Eventually I had to face the reality: Edward had clearly developed an unhealthy dependence on my instruction and did not want to move on. Hard as it was, I had to terminate his lessons.

Lesson structures for nervous riders

Establishing the basics

In many ways, fear and respect are two sides of the same coin. Both denote an awareness of the horse's power; one in a way that makes us feel powerless, the other in a way that makes us feel more in control. Without having felt fear in the first place, some people unfortunately don't develop the necessary respect to handle horses responsibly. However, a growth in confidence should be managed with the same care as the dissolution of fear. Just as there is a fine line between a lack of confidence and fear, there can be an even finer line between a return to confidence and the emergence of arrogance. Therefore, the lesson structures I am putting forward to help nervous riders should be applied thoughtfully to the differing circumstances of each student rather than followed slavishly.

Certain approaches to the management of fear suggested here will appeal to certain riders but not to others. Some will work more quickly for a particular personality type; others will benefit from them only over time.

The methods chosen and the time spent employing these methods will, and indeed should, vary according to the degree of the student's fear. A mere lapse in confidence may be dealt with by the shorter-term use of these exercises, while outright and absolute terror will require a long-term approach and commitment to their dedicated application. Instructors on all levels should try to remain as flexible as possible and be prepared to try different approaches to the same problem, including variations on the methods suggested here, providing they retain a constant awareness of safety precautions at all times.

A useful approach for relieving the high expectations that might result from starting this programme is to remember there should be no time scale set for the resolution of fear. Not only does that put unnecessary pressure on

> Without having felt fear in the first place, some people never develop the respect to handle horses responsibly.

an already stressed rider but it might also preclude the possibility of resolving the situation earlier. Rather, regard fear as a phenomenon that will dissolve when the rider is ready to let go of it, which is usually as soon as she has been equipped with the knowledge, confidence and practical methods to deal with it.

Despite the wisdom of not regarding the management of fear as something that can be achieved with quick fixes, some riders do experience a sudden, strong return of confidence that surpasses expectations. Some can even become overconfident. When this happens, be most cautious: try to temper this boldness into a sensible confidence without allowing the student to slip back into fear. This is not the time for daring exploits and for testing the limits of such newfound courage. Under no circumstances should the rider be allowed to do something that might endanger her life or that of the horse, or cause a relapse of fear.

Throughout the application of this rehabilitation programme, inspire confidence in your ability to help your students by being honest with them about their progress. If you are able to detect in them sabotaging behaviour that is impeding progress, draw their attention to it. Diplomacy, especially in the case of novices and the nervous, is fine, but blatant lies just to keep a pupil happy are not.

The following suggested lesson structures are for instructors and riders who have access to school horses who are both sound and trustworthy!

Lesson one

- Begin the lesson by establishing the student's primary fear and its probable cause. Assure the rider that her seemingly irrational fear is a positive emotion in the sense that it can be turned into a healthy respect for horses.

- Remind the student that it is natural, not 'naughty', for horses to want to act independently but that it is possible to cultivate the appropriate horsemanship skills to prevent the horse from becoming dangerous in its quest for dominance.

- Assure the student that she will be taught a variety of approaches and instructed in practical ways to handle a horse so that the event feared is less likely to occur or reoccur.

- Discuss with the student the safety value of appropriate riding attire. If necessary, provide set guidelines for acceptable wear. Recommend the clothing most likely to protect against injury or lessen the severity of an injury. Ensure that the student wears protective headgear during lessons, even if they entail only groundwork exercises.

- Regardless of the student's previous riding experience or ability, conduct the entire lesson without allowing any actual riding. Explain to the student that to be able to control a horse effectively from its back, control should first be achieved safely on the ground.

- Prior to allowing any handling that involves close contact with the horse, ensure that the student is very familiar with how to move around in a manner that will neither endanger her nor the horse.

- Help the student enforce ground manners from the horse.

- Introduce or re-introduce the student to ground handling the horse. Instruct her to perform ground-handling exercises and grooming

Suggested ground manner checks using a 3-4m (12ft) lead rope include:

1 **Respectful waiting:** Let the horse stand calmly and wait for the handler's cue before leaving or entering stables, round pens, arenas and paddocks. Get the horse in this 'waiting-for-you' frame of mind by opening the stable door or gate fully and insisting that he faces it calmly and does not move towards it without the appropriate command. Reinforce this by stopping the horse and backing him up every time he makes an unasked – for move.

2 **Respectful distance:** Enforce a respectful distance of at least a metre or yard when leading the horse. The desirable distance is communicated to the horse by halting him and backing him up whenever he gets too close or tries to lead the handler. Strive to do all leading with a loose rein. Whenever the horse becomes 'stuck' on the ground, don't pull ineffectively on the lead rope but move off to the side, gently tugging on the lead rope so that the horse has to move his feet to retain his balance.

3 **Respectful manners:** 'Send' the horse through a stable or gate ahead of you on a long lead rope. Teaching a horse to lead in this manner minimizes the risks of you getting crushed against a stable door or a paddock gate, or getting trampled.

4 **Respectful obedience:** Stop the horse frequently on voice command. If he doesn't respond or takes too long, stop him with the halter and back him up to the spot where the command to halt was originally given.

5 **Respectful attention:** Lead the horse to the centre of an enclosed area, stay next to him within his sight and release pressure on the lead rope. When he moves his head at all, give a gentle pull on the lead rope to bring him back to the original position you placed him in. Do this for about ten minutes at a time. The horse will eventually learn how to remain aware of his surroundings without having to turn his head, thereby never losing the silent thread of command from you, the handler.

Suggested ground-handling exercises include:

1 **Disengageent:** Ask the horse to 'step over' with the hind legs to ensure that he will be able to disengage his hindquarters in an emergency in order to reduce power.

2 **Suppleness:** Flex the neck laterally both ways to check that the horse is supple enough to respond to a shortening of the rein on one side to reduce his reach and speed should you need to pull him up quickly.

3 **Submission:** Flex the head laterally to check that the horse can lower his head in submission to the handler.

4 **Soundness:** Check the horse's back for possible injury by massaging the spine and rotating the tail to ensure that it is not immovably clamped between the buttocks with tension.

5 **Calmness:** Check that the horse is relaxed by carefully feeling the area behind its flank, namely the section of skin where the hind leg joins the body and forms a loose triangle. If this is soft and 'stretchy' when the student hooks a finger or two behind and gently pulls, it is a good sign. If the flanks are unyielding and tense like wire, the groundwork exercises should be repeated again until the horse relaxes enough to be ridden safely.

whenever possible from next to the horse's shoulder, a position from where she enjoys the best possible protection.

• With the student, devise further exercises to address her particular concerns. If the student, for instance, has had a bad experience with a horse getting his legs caught in wire or another constrictive type of device that caused him to panic and sustain injury, work together to accustom the horse to 'losing' a leg, yet remain calm. A way to do this is to take the lead rope and rub it over the horse's legs before looping it behind one leg (above the pastern) and picking it up, holding it firm for a few seconds before releasing.

- Don't try and cram every possible aspect of ground manners or groundwork into this lesson. If the entire session is taken up with successfully teaching the student to keep a horse at a respectful distance while leading him, something worthwhile has been achieved.
- Unless the student brings along somebody for moral support, don't allow uninvited spectators to witness the lesson. Most nervous riders find an audience intimidating and distracting.
- Try and finish the lesson on a high note, with the student having achieved a small measure of confidence in her ability to control a horse on the ground.
- Compliment the student on each valid achievement, but don't overdo it. She may be nervous, but will still be able to tell the difference between genuine appreciation for effort and false praise.

Lesson two

- Repeat all the steps from the previous lessons. Don't introduce any new work until both you and the student truthfully believe that those basic horsemanship skills have been mastered.

- Introduce those steps of the ground manners and groundwork that were not covered in the first lesson.

- If there is time at the end of the session, let the student just sit quietly on the horse for a couple of minutes without moving off. If this opportunity arises, emphasize to the student the vital importance of not mounting or dismounting a horse unless he is standing completely still. This quiet time can be used to give the student advice on her seat and the ideal position of her hands and legs.

- Impress upon her the importance of patience in establishing or re-establishing trust between human and horse, as well as the non-negotiable necessity of acquiring every possible skill that could enhance the safety and confidence of both horse and rider.

Lesson three

- Confirm the ground manners and groundwork as before. If the student is able to perform all these exercises with confidence, allow her to give the horse a thorough grooming. This is an excellent time to observe whether she is keeping a keen eye on the horse for any signs of distress or any other attempts to communicate something important, like a sore back, to the handler.

- Allow the student to turn the horse out. Teach her to set him free in a controlled and safe manner, ensuring that he remains standing calmly for a while after the halter is removed. Instruct the student to step away from the horse first, thereby giving him 'permission' to go.

- Task the student to sit quietly nearby and observe the horse's behaviour, including his reaction to and interaction with other horses. Use subsequent feedback to explain the importance of hierarchy in the herd and how the horse carries over that struggle for supremacy to his relationship with humans.

- If there is time, let the student catch the horse herself. Make sure she knows not to persist in approaching the horse if he has turned his back to her in a disrespectful and possibly threatening manner. Teach the student how to 'turn' the horse, first from a safe distance, with body movements and voice aids.

Lesson four

- Begin this lesson by confirming that the student has a thorough understanding of the tack used on the horse and knowledge of how to maintain it.

- Repeat the groundwork and ground manner exercises from the previous lessons.

- If the student is ready to ride, introduce her to some fear-busting exercises on the horse's back, but end the lesson without having given the rider control of the horse.

The following tasks are useful for developing confidence in Lesson 4:

1 **Relieve the student of control**: Halter the horse and begin by leading the student around on him in an enclosed arena or area. Some adults may baulk at this apparent 'babying' by their instructors, but usually only if they don't yet understand the relevance of the exercise in eventually helping them deal with their fears. Allow the student to hold on to the saddle-horn, pommel or a neck strap. Don't let her become discouraged if she can only manage a few short strides at first. The major benefit of this exercise is that it relieves nervous riders of the responsibility of having to control the horse and gives them a chance to learn to relax on horseback. Move to a more open area when the student is ready to progress.

2 **Ask for a leap of faith:** Once the student is feeling more comfortable, ask her to close her eyes for short periods of time while being led so as to be able to concentrate fully on becoming 'part' of the horse by absorbing his movement through her hips and lower back. Once the student is able to 'synchronize' her movements with those of the horse, she will be able to feel quickly and distinctly how one 'gets behind' the motion whenever tension seizes the body and robs it of its suppleness.

3 **Play a game:** This task can progress to the rider being asked to guess which of the horse's feet is touching the ground and at what moment. This helps a nervous student to focus on a job rather than on her own fear. When she eventually starts doing more advanced work, it will also ensure that she can time her cues correctly to achieve a square stop.

4 **Set a challenge:** As the student's confidence grows, invite her to lift the balls of her feet off the treads of the stirrups without pulling them out altogether. Once the feet are not pressing into the stirrups for balance, ask her to start 'finding' her seat in the saddle by concentrating on balancing on the seat bones instead of on the pubic bone or the coccyx.

Lesson five

- Repeat the ground manners and groundwork exercises. By now the student should be able to do each step without lengthy repetitions being necessary.

- If the previous lesson didn't allow time for all the fear-busting exercises, introduce those tasks now. Otherwise repeat them in full.

Lesson six

- Confirm the student's ground manner and groundwork skills and repeat the fear-busting exercises.

- Providing the student is steadily gaining in confidence, this might be the appropriate stage to prepare her for taking up the reins. To do this, use the challenges detailed below.

Further challenges

1 **Develop balance:** While leading the student, ask her to stop holding on to the pommel or horn of the saddle and let her hands rest lightly on her middle thigh. Regular practice of this should prevent her from balancing herself on the reins once she takes them up.

2 **Use the single rein:** A more advanced exercise for checking the hands don't overreact is to task the student to take up the single lead rein herself. Ask the student to halt the horse every few paces to ensure that she is in full control, and feels being so. Instruct the student in directional control, explaining and encouraging the use of leg aids to turn the horse instead of 'pulling' him around or over-using the lead rein.

By the successful conclusion of this exercise, the student should be ready to actually take up the reins.

Lesson seven

- Repeat all the relevant steps from previous lessons.

- For the first proper riding session, keep the student in an enclosed area and insist that she keeps the horse at a walk. Explain the necessity of being able to do all ridden work correctly and calmly at a walk before attempting it at a faster pace.

- This is an appropriate time for the instructor to introduce the student to an emergency or one-rein stop. Let her practise turning the horse in a circle at a walk (ensuring the crossing of the hind legs) to reduce speed instead of pulling back on the reins. This 'gearing-down' exercise is useful in as far as it gives the rider the psychological boost associated with the discovery that she can slow down and stop the horse without having to rely on physical strength.

- Once the instructor is satisfied that the student feels in control of the horse at a walk inside the pen or arena, an outride can be attempted. The horse should still be kept at a walk and the student accompanied by at least one other experienced and able rider. On this ride and the next few, remember to take a halter along in case of a sudden lapse in confidence.

Further lessons and confidence tests

When a high level of confidence has been achieved, begin or return to instructing according to the rider's actual abilities and the requirements of the discipline she wishes to follow. If she is cooperative, suggest that for several weeks, months even, all work should be undertaken at a walk. Use follow-up lessons to set confidence tests in order to measure the growth in her ability in handling horses and the level of submission such handling can effect in a horse.

In order to properly test the rider, the instructor will have to purposely create circumstances most likely to result in slight reluctance in the horse to obey the rider's wishes. It goes without saying that only a trustworthy schoolmaster should be used, a horse with the type of temperament that would produce only token resistance to unfamiliar challenges and mishandling.

The following scenarios could be used to set confidence tests for students:

O **Confidence test 1: Introduce the student to a new horse.**

It is always in the best interest of a nervous rider to see that she regains her confidence on as many different horses as are safely available. This prevents students from having their newfound security tied up in a single horse and having a relapse into fear when presented with an unfamiliar one.

O **Confidence test 2: Task the student to ride out alone.**

If the student is still lacking in the necessary confidence, the horse could display a barn-sour (nappy) attitude by being reluctant to leave. Should the student appear intimidated by the horse taking advantage of her uncertainty, don't let the situation escalate to the point where she relapses into fear or gets into a futile power struggle. Rather, set out on the ride with her to break the deadlock. Once the student has managed to successfully leave the stableyard area in your company, ride away from her, beginning with short distances and gradually increasing them, to allow her and her horse to build confidence without panicking.

O Confidence test 3: Expose the rider to a new environment.

Both horse and rider can become 'route-bound' if they continually follow the same predictable route. If there is no alternative, create the impression of one by turning around when you get close to the yard, going up cul de sacs or riding around a tree instead of just past it. Putting horse and rider through a 'new' experience together is a great way of building trust between them.

O Confidence test 4: Ask the rider to 'override' the horse's herd instincts.

Every time you and your student ride out together, impress upon her the absolute necessity of not allowing her horse to follow into the gaits of other horses without express commands to do so. Infractions should be dealt with immediately by halting the horse and backing him up a little, or turning him in a small circle every time he wants to go forward until he can stand calmly, waiting for a cue from his rider. By confirming that the student is able to condition the horse to change gaits only when the appropriate cue has been given, the instructor helps prevent her from becoming the type of rider whose lack of control over her horse endangers herself and fellow riders.

O Confidence test 5: Task the student to set new parameters for the horse.

Ask the student to ride the horse some distance past the barn or stable yard, his stall or the tie-rail, in fact past any and all of the familiar places where the horse customarily ends his training or outride. This will reinforce in the student's mind the absolute wisdom of avoiding behavioural patterns that will allow the horse to predict exactly when his work for the day will be finished or at what point the rider will dismount and unsaddle him. By not allowing the horse to develop set expectations, potentially dangerous insistence on his part to have them met can be prevented.

○ Confidence test 6: Task the student to ask the horse for an encore.

Occasionally let the student take the horse out twice in a row and return only when the horse is moving out willingly. On arrival at the unsaddling point, the student should remain in the saddle if the horse shows any signs of impatience, such as pawing the ground. By not allowing the horse to expect a certain limit on his use, he is less likely to put up serious resistance when being asked to perform extra work.

○ Confidence test 7: Do the unexpected with the horse.

Another effective way of testing the student's confidence in asking the horse for something and remaining firm when he becomes resistant, is to instruct her to saddle and mount her horse and just sit calmly while other horses are being ridden away, ridden past, arriving back at the yard or the barn, or being unsaddled and turned out. Every time her horse tries to move off, the student should be ready and willing to stop him, back him up, and then ride him forward again to the exact spot where the exercise began.

These exercises are as much a discipline for the rider as for the horse. They are certainly not the only possible confidence tests we could set our students in order to assess their ability, and instructors should use their particular environment to improvise and develop further tasks to help expand positive behavioural patterns that are likely to enhance confidence and safety prospects. Even when students pass all their confidence tests with ease, some or all of them should be reintroduced into their lessons on a regular basis. This will ensure that the rider doesn't lose confidence again or becomes intimidated by possible new levels of resistance in the horse.

> Confidence tests are a necessary
> discipline for both horse and rider.

case study

Rising to the challenge...

It was a quite intense fear of falling from a horse that brought Paul, a martial artist, to me for confidence training. He had no history of horrible accidents. In fact, he had no history with horses at all; just the desire to be able to ride, but being prevented from even trying by his own incapacitating fear of being dislodged and dumped in a pitiful heap by the roadside.

An important part of my work with him was convincing him that he already possessed one of the most important qualities needed to prevent just such an occurrence. That asset was the enviable physical balance he had achieved through many years of training in and teaching martial arts. Apart from the groundwork and ground manner skills students are always taught, Paul's first sessions also incorporated those exercises most likely to convince him that he was indeed centred enough on the horse to greatly reduce the chances of him simply falling off. These began with him being led around on horseback at varying speeds without being allowed to hold on to the reins in order to prevent him from trying to balance himself on them.

As Paul's belief in his balance grew, so the exercises became more challenging. For instance, I would halt the horse suddenly or turn it unexpectedly to test the balance he would be likely to display if a horse shied with him. In each case Paul exhibited only temporary loss of balance by either tipping slightly forwards, backwards or sideways during the unexpected manoeuvres. While I initially did not ask him to take his feet out of the stirrups, I encouraged him to try and ride without pressing them down hard in an attempt to maintain balance.

Within a few lessons, Paul was happy to submit himself to these balance-enhancing challenges with his eyes closed. Within weeks, his faith in his own ability to stay on had become firm enough for him to declare that he was ready for 'normal' riding lessons. Since then his riding ability has grown steadily, and he is even contemplating taking part in shows at sometime in the future.

Practical responses to the most common fears

As we have already established, the majority of people respond better if they are given practical and workable suggestions to help them cope with a frightening situation, rather than simply being told not to worry. Most would actually find such a suggestion singularly unhelpful if not backed up by appropriate and applicable advice. The only effective long-term answer to fear relating to horses and riding situations remains the implementation of practical counter-measures and workable solutions. These give the handler and rider 'real' options to manage fear, and help convince her that she is growing in her ability to control horses and her feelings regarding them.

Advice should include specific suggestions as to how to prevent or remedy situations such as the following:

Bolting

A rider who fears bolting should be taught the 'one-rein stop'. This emergency procedure is executed not by instinctively pulling back with equal force on both reins (often futile), but by increasingly shortening one rein to turn the horse in a circle, starting with a big arc so as not to pull him off balance, and slowly decreasing the size of the circles until he is 'geared down' to the extent that he stops.

Mastering the one-rein stop usually reduces the rider's level of fear to the extent that she transfers much less apprehension to the horse, which in turn calms him, thereby decreasing the likelihood of an unfortunate chain of events being set in motion that could culminate in a serious accident.

Kicking

It is quite astonishing how many people, especially non-riders, perceive horses as being naturally disposed to kicking. Yet, apart from mares in a 'protect-the-womb' mood or bad-tempered stallions and geldings, few horses will kick out without provocation. When they do, it is usually a defensive reaction to a human action.

Students who fear being kicked, and even those who do not, should be taught how to prevent what could be a defensive action by observing certain rules, especially with regard to the correct distance when moving around horses; contrary to popular opinion, the safest place to be in order to avoid being kicked is right up against the horse. This entails moving around the hindquarters so closely as to almost rub against them, while keeping one hand on the rump and continually talking to the horse.

A good groundwork exercise for people who are fearful of being kicked is to teach them to handle the horse's feet and clean the hooves. Although this cannot prevent them from being kicked if they move carelessly around a horse, doing so usually helps them get a sense of control over the object of their fear.

case study

Fear of kicking and losing control…

Andrew, a psychologist, was afraid not only of riding horses, but of handling them, too. He came for lessons to overcome this fear because he desperately wanted to share his wife's passion for riding. By then, a handful of previous attempts to deal with his concerns by simply 'getting on and going' had resulted in 'terror rides' at various stable yards.

His wife despaired of Andrew ever mastering his fear sufficiently to enjoy being with horses. Nevertheless, she went ahead with plans to buy her own horse and stable it at their home. Andrew's desire to be able to help her care for and even exercise the horse should the need arise, inspired him to try one last time to deal with his fears.

During our first lesson I determined that Andrew's fear of horses was not merely generalized unease, but was very specific in that he worried about being kicked by a horse when handling it and of losing control while riding it. In this case I felt it prudent to first help him deal with his fear of being kicked before moving on to those fears that plagued him about actually riding. I began by assuring him that there were indeed certain ways of moving around a horse that could greatly minimize the handler's risk of being kicked. The hardest part for him was to believe that he really could be safe while stepping around the horse with his body right up against the animal. But after a few minutes of repeatedly moving around the horse in this manner without being harmed, Andrew started relaxing. It was then possible to introduce him to physically handling the horse's hooves, first the front feet a number of times until he felt reassured enough to pick up the back feet. By the end of the first half of the lesson, he was able to clean the hooves without becoming panic-stricken: actually holding the horse's hooves in his hands gave him a sense of control not only over the horse's most dangerous weapon, but over his own fears as well.

Biting

As in the case of kicking, many people erroneously believe that biting is something that a horse will just do. They don't realize, however, that many horses are unwittingly 'encouraged' if not 'taught' by humans to do so.

In order to reduce the chances of being nipped by a horse, students should be discouraged from hand-feeding titbits and from playing with the muzzle as this could teach a horse to eventually demand treats in a potentially dangerous way. Carrots, apples and flavoured biscuits alike should

hold the thought

Teach students to stay positioned at the horse's shoulder when handling the animal. It is the safest place to be.

be put in feed bins. Students should also be made aware of the fact that horses that try and bite under circumstances unrelated to feeding habits, are displaying disrespectful behaviour to the humans around them. Often the best way to convey to them that their behaviour is unacceptable is to 'bite back' instantly, using fingers to simulate teeth. The best place to leave the 'don't-bite-me' message is on the horse's neck, as seen in the herd situation when horses retaliate.

Riders should also learn to keep themselves out of the horse's temptation zone; this means keeping themselves positioned at the horse's shoulder at all times when handling the animal. This is the safest place to be when around a horse as it prevents one from becoming a target not only for the teeth, but also for the head, a proverbial sledgehammer at the best of times.

Bucking

It is said that horses are so honest they will give 'warning' before they do something that may hurt us. This is often too true in the case of horses that 'suddenly' buck. Bucking may be a response to some discomfort and students should be taught how to detect all possible early warning signs by carrying out a few simple checks prior to saddling and riding.

The back should be checked for signs of soreness by massaging the horse along the spine. If he flinches at any particular point or if the handler has troubling lifting and rotating the tail, where the lower part of the spine is located, the horse is not going to be comfortable under saddle and should preferably not be ridden until he recovers sufficiently to not mind being pressed along the spine. Another place a prospective rider should examine before mounting the horse is the flanks. If they are soft and yielding, the horse is relaxed; if they are tight and tense, the horse should be worked on the ground instead of being saddled until he relaxes sufficiently to be ridden.

Educate students on the vital importance of having a 'bucking' horse examined by a qualified equine chiropractor, a dentist, a veterinarian, or all three if necessary, to determine whether the cause of the horse's behaviour is physical in nature. In addition, point out that it may be advisable to consult an animal nutritionist to investigate the possibility of the problem being feed-related.

Once all possible physical causes have been ruled out, the rider may have to accept that it is her handling of the animal that has caused it to resort to bucking to avoid carrying out her wishes. Such riders should be encouraged to return to the basics outlined in the suggested lesson plans until they are confident they have addressed the situation.

Rearing

Novice and nervous riders should be strongly discouraged from riding or owning horses that have reared with them or that have a history of rearing. Nervous riders who have not experienced rearing, but are afraid of this happening, should be taught to ride with light hands so as not to cause unnecessary pain in the mouth of the horse, a factor likely to contribute to the vice. They should also be repeatedly conditioned, that should a horse ever rear with them, not to hang on to the reins as this could have the effect of pulling the animal over, possibly on top of them.

Early on in their instruction, students should be made aware that many nervous riders unwittingly encourage horses to rear by kicking them to go, while at the same time holding them back for fear of moving off too fast. When a rider does this, the horse has only one way to go and that is up, and often over.

hold the thought

Nervous riders should be told which actions could unwittingly encourage frightening behaviour in horses.

Falling

Good balance and an independent seat are invaluable aids in staying on top of a horse when it spooks, bucks, rears or bolts.

Many people have excellent natural balance or participate in sports that help develop it, but those who are not so lucky need to be reminded to make a conscious effort to balance on their seat bones, instead of on the reins and in the stirrups. To help students develop a balanced seat, some basic instruction in classical riding as well as lessons on the lunge can be extremely valuable. Once the rider realizes that she can stay on the horse without literally 'holding on for dear life', the fear of falling off usually lessens.

Loss of control

Many riders who fear they are powerless to maintain or regain control of a horse have simply never been taught how to do so.

In order for the student to believe that she could either prevent or cope with a loss of control, she should learn the necessary horse-handling skills to enable her to do so.

Begin by asking the student to practise stopping the horse every few steps, first on the ground, then in an enclosed area while riding at a walk, and then during an outride. Every time the horse moves off without a cue from the rider, ask her to halt again, back up and keep him standing still until he calmly awaits further instruction.

Fear of the horse not obeying commands

Novice and fearful riders frequently encounter resistance in the horse to carry out their requests precisely because it can sense they are afraid of the very thing they are asking it to do. This situation can only be remedied by the rider ensuring that cues are given in the same unambiguous manner every time, and with enough authority to be taken seriously.

Lack of authority can present a rider or handler with immense problems. The horse will recognize when authority is lacking or absent and will act accordingly. Too often, we lose our authority by regarding and treating horses as pets, thus negating their potential power and dignity. Such romantic indulgence could have serious safety implications as this inappropriate handling gives rise to disrespect in the horse and reluctance to accept authority. Consequently, the horse is more likely to challenge the rider on every occasion and show reluctance in obeying commands. By developing a realistic attitude towards horses and their immense power, riders can help prevent situations where their authority is undermined and their requests ignored.

case study

Consistency and authority... Arabella, an ex-model, received a beautiful horse from her husband as a birthday present. What she had never mentioned to him was that she had had some horrific horse-riding accidents in her youth, one leaving her in a coma for several days. During conversations with Arabella, it became clear that most of the accidents she had been involved in resulted from rebellious behaviour on the part of her horses, directly or indirectly brought on, or aggravated by, her inconsistent handling of them. For instance, she had been bucked off numerous times and even had a horse rear over backwards with her in defiance of her erratic commands. It emerged that she would repeatedly allow a horse to nap and turn back to the stable yard, and then abruptly insist that it leave on a trail ride.

On observing Arabella around horses, it quickly became obvious from the

Treating horses as pets gives rise to
disrespect and has serious safety
implications for the rider.

way she baby-talked to them and her own apologetic body language when approaching and handling them, that she did not have the necessary respect for their power. In fact, that type of well-intentioned indulgence had the potential to turn a horse 'dangerous' by allowing, encouraging and rewarding unacceptable behaviour. Arabella needed to go back to basics and master the firm, but calm and consistent handling methods needed to obtain respect from a horse on the ground before she allowed herself to get back to riding and expect the horse to pay attention to her commands. Consistency and authority were key issues she had to address.

Unfortunately she baulked at having to do 'such silly stuff', declaring that she would feel much too embarrassed to be seen in my 'kindergarten', and didn't return for the next lesson. Several months later, however, she did come back. She admitted that she had become so intimidated by her horse that she was too fearful to even try and correct his unwanted behaviour. Putting aside her concerns about what other people might think of her doing such a basic programme, she committed herself to long-term work on her attitude towards horses. She has made progress and is still taking lessons …

A general fear of horses

Some people are so afraid of horses that they become panic-stricken even in their mere vicinity. But if they still have a sincere desire to one day be able to ride a horse without being afraid, introduce them to the horse's environment by using a step-by-step approach that will desensitize them slowly but effectively.

Start by teaching them how to tackle stable chores, all activities that will bring them into close, but not direct, contact with horses. They can then be taught how to behave around horses on the ground in order to remain as safe as possible. Progress to horse care, encouraging them to spend as much time as they want grooming a particular horse, and then as many as possible to best experience the calming effect it can have on both animal and handler.

Continue to reinforce all these activities without putting pressure on the student to start riding. Only when she expresses a strong desire to be taught how to ride a horse, should actual riding lessons commence.

These routines are also particularly useful for people who have no intention of riding horses, but find themselves in a position of having to help their children or others in handling them.

Consider teaching the student how to lunge a horse. Ensure that she understands the principles of lungeing as well as its proper purpose, and doesn't come to regard it merely as the quickest and easiest way to tire the horse out before the rider gets on.

Also teach the student how to communicate with the horse during lungeing and what aspects of the horse's carriage and movement to pay particular attention to. This will prevent her from performing the lungeing as a meaningless exercise.

The student could even be taught how to use body language to effect directional control of a free horse in a round pen, learning how to drive the horse forward by putting pressure on its hindquarters and turning it in the opposite direction by stepping sideways and forward to 'block' it with pressure on the shoulder.

hold the thought

Even non-riding horse lovers should be taught how to behave around horses to remain as safe as possible.

Dealing with the relapse: a recurrence of fear

It is possible to manage fear. It is possible to transform fear into respect.
It is not possible, however, to guarantee that it will never return again.
Like happiness and anger, fear too can be triggered again at any time in
the future, in its full intensity.

Despite an instructor's best efforts at training students to become, and
remain, riders who practise sound horsemanship principles, there is simply
no guarantee that they will never again find themselves in the paralyzing grip
of fear. Should this happen, whether the fear returns in a mild or severe
form, whether because of an unfortunate accident or for a completely
inexplicable reason, there is only one solution if the student is still serious
about continuing with her riding: go back to the beginning.

This is when a student simply has to be prepared to allow the instructor to
restart the process of methodically implementing practical ways to minimize
the chances of such fears being realized or recurring again.

Anybody who has put themselves through the process of fear management
once usually finds that it works even better and faster the second time
around. When a rider has to be 'restarted' because of recurring fear, it can be
most useful if, at all possible, the exact cause of the relapse can be isolated.
This should give the instructor additional help in deciding on the best
possible route of redeveloping respect for the horse as opposed to
counteracting the fear of it.

In addition to practising the recommended fear-busting exercises
contained in the lessons, and going through the mandatory safety procedures
when handling and riding the horse, the rider could also implement
additional remedial procedures should the following scenarios occur.

O **Careless behaviour on the part of a riding companion.**
Advise the rider not to go out riding with that person again. She should not be embarrassed to explain in firm terms that the other person's behaviour on horseback was threatening to her. Students should be exhorted to remember that their physical safety is always more important than their popularity with other riders.

O **Witnessing or hearing about an accident.**
Remind the student that such mishaps are never 100 per cent preventable. More importantly, re-emphasize that she does know how to practise safe and responsible horse handling and riding, and that she already possesses the very means to minimize the chances of something unfortunate happening to her.

O **Involvement in an accident.**
If an accident occurred because of the rider using an aid or giving a cue incorrectly, do corrective instruction with the student in the next lesson. Also put the student and the horse repeatedly through the fear-busting exercises from the first lessons until their confidence returns strongly.

O **Overconfidence.**
If fear has been rekindled because of the rider neglecting her horsemanship or safety principles during a bout of too much newfound confidence, help her to find a balance between actions on horseback that lack firmness because of the presence of fear and those that are too exaggerated because of its absence. Students must realize that a lack of fear does not compensate for a lack of skill, and that horses handled inexpertly could display dangerous resistance, rekindling fear in the rider once again.

Safety mantra

At this point it may be useful for the instructor and the student to sit down together and draw up a 'safety mantra', a list of daily practices, the regular implementation of which should further prevent situations likely to trigger a recurrence of fear. While there is no single blueprint for what constitutes the perfect horseman, there are riding habits we can acquire, exercises we can routinely do and behaviours we can avoid, all of which help us to become safer and more confident around horses. These ought to become the horsemanship tenets that the rider should endeavour to implement on an ongoing basis to effect the safest possible enjoyment of horse riding.

A 'headline' version of the list, such as the one suggested overleaf, could be written up and placed in the tack room, stable yard or in any other spot where students can read it regularly, preferably prior to having contact with the horse. The instructor could also go through each point on a regular basis as a progressive aid to developing understanding and confidence.

At no point should we allow ourselves, or those for whose well-being we are responsible, to become careless about safety once fear has been relinquished. We should also never countenance arrogance in the newly fear-less as it could be but a precursor to irresponsible actions that could cause the return of fear.

Ultimately, the most reasonable expectations we should have of our riding is a feeling of contentment at our growing ability, gratitude to be safe, and joy at being privileged to enjoy nature on such a magnificent beast.

hold the thought

Practise a regime of safety around horses. It is this maintenance of responsibility that keeps fear at bay.

○ Don't 'catch' or transfer fear: refrain from listening to or passing on horror stories.

○ Don't frighten the horse: remember that horses are sensitive to your feelings and will pick up on them.

○ Don't 'over-horse' yourself: never allow yourself to be paired with a highly strung horse.

○ Master ground control: practise the appropriate ground manner, and groundwork exercises before mounting.

○ Translate your groundwork into your riding: when mounted, correct your horse in the same way as you would on the ground.

○ Ask – don't force: use natural and artificial aids correctly and sensitively.

○ Be consistent: consistency is the most effective way to set acceptable limits on the horse's behaviour.

○ Remember that a horse is not a pet: develop a realistic attitude towards horses and their immense power.

○ Take time to build trust: once achieved, trust cannot be taken for granted and needs to be nurtured constantly.

○ Remember that bravado on horseback is not horsemanship: never allow yourself to be bullied or shamed on to a horse that is not suitable for you.

○ Don't ride with your ego: be secure in your level of ability.

4
Hypnotherapy for the Nervous Rider

Sharon Shinwell

'Our unconscious mind sometimes stores data that prevents us from reaching our goals. Hypnotherapy is an effective means of allowing the unconscious mind to be spoken to. During hypnosis positive ideas, feelings and thoughts are taken on board willingly, replacing negative ones that hold us back. The conscious mind adopts these and we feel, think and behave differently. The calm and confident feeling this creates opens up a whole new world for the nervous rider.'

Dispelling the myths about hypnosis

As riders, we are all subject to the onset of nerves from time to time. An attack may be short-lived or a long-term, debilitating problem. Hypnotherapy can be a great aid to the nervous rider at these times. It can help us to re-programme our unconscious mind, allowing it to reconnect with our conscious one, in order to reduce or even remove whatever blockage is stopping us from achieving our goals with our horses.

Most of you will be familiar with those stage hypnotists seen on television and in the media. Hypnosis has had a confused history because of the myth and folk law associated with it, and it has been the tool of charlatans and entertainers for many years. Clinical hypnotherapy, however, is quite another matter and is by no means a new phenomenon. In fact the use of hypnotherapy and hypnosis to solve emotional and psychological problems dates back as far as 1779.

My own experience of the effectiveness of hypnotherapy occurred after many years of fearful involvement with horses. If I had only known then what I know now, I might have been able to combat my own fears and anxieties before a back injury got there first.

case study

Personal experience Having always ridden quiet riding-school horses in my youth and possessing the self-assured feeling of immortality that only the under twenty-ones have in large doses, it became a bit of a different story once I had become a responsible adult and mother. It suddenly dawned on me that riding could be potentially dangerous, in fact life threatening! The problem for me was that no one else I knew in my circle of 'horsey' friends seemed to suffer with this same gut-wrenching realization, or if they had, they were keeping it to themselves.

I changed my horse three times in as many years and had numerous lessons and coaching sessions from some very well-respected experts, yet still I made

> The unconscious mind can be changed and when this happens the possibilities are endless.

excuse after excuse as to why I wasn't achieving my potential. Only I knew what the issue really was: I was terrified of riding and sometimes of even handling my horse. I had been through a few nasty experiences while learning the ropes of horse ownership, and some nastier ones having bred a foal, and these clouded every thought I had when it came to dealing with the present. Even when I had found my 'ideal' horse and finally got off the bottom rungs on the dressage ladder, I still felt physically sick at the thought of tacking up and riding. When I think about it now, I can so easily relive those feelings of sheer panic and fear; the anxiety of knowing that to continue with this hobby, I had to ride. I can still hear the words my husband use to fling at me when his patience ran out and frustration took over, 'What are we paying all this money out for?' and I knew he was right. But horses get into your blood and the whole way of life that surrounds them is a difficult one to leave.

At that time I didn't know about hypnotherapy and hypnosis. I didn't realize that the conscious and unconscious mind could be at odds with one another, and that once the mind had taken control, the body soon followed. I was unaware that you could actually change how you thought about something without being consciously aware that you had. Once I had learned this, a whole new world opened up.

Because I have never forgotten those times of dread and fear, helping others to overcome their own negative thoughts, feelings and behaviours, and changing them into a positive experience, seemed a natural step to take and I have used hypnotherapy to help many riders overcome their fears. I now know just how complicated and complex we are as a species and when it comes to trying to understand the mind and how it works, the learning process never stops. It's time this absorbing world of horse riding gave back to its nervous participants as much pleasure as they devote time and energy to looking after their mounts.

Schools of thought

We are still learning about how the mind works as opposed to the brain, and although clinical hypnotherapists have been practising for a long time, even to this day there are still a number of theories as to what the state of hypnosis actually is and how it works.

I was taught the model of hypnotherapy developed by Milton H. Erickson MD. The foundation of Erickson's hypnotherapeutic system is his assumption that people have both a conscious mind and an unconscious mind. Erickson used the term 'unconscious mind' to refer to all the cognitions, perceptions and emotions which occur outside a person's normal range of awareness, and reserved the term 'conscious mind' for the limited range of information that enters the restricted focus of attention of most people in everyday life.

There are many other schools of thought adopted by practitioners, including Disassociation, Atavistic, Hyper-suggestibility and Altered State Theories to name but a few, and there are some excellent books available if you really want to get your teeth into the subject in some depth. Suffice to say that recent developments have resulted in a common view that the 'state of hypnosis' is both scientific and phenomenological.

Will it work for me?

With so many theories abounding you can understand why it is so difficult to answer just in a few words when people ask me, 'How does it work?' – but then I guess what you really want to know is, 'Will it work for me?' as you strive to overcome your fears of riding. Like all alternative and complementary therapies, there are no guarantees (there again, the medical profession is not so good at giving those, either!) but if you have an open mind and an imagination, there is every chance it will do.

It is generally accepted that 90 percent of the population can be induced into the hypnotic trance state by an individual hypnotherapist, provided that the subject is willing and unafraid. Analytically minded people who try to work out

> Be open-minded and there is every chance hypnotherapy will work for you.

the whys and wherefores of what is happening to them during hypnotherapy are not likely to find the process as easy to relax into as others, but even for these people, sufficient depth of the hypnotic state for successful treatment can be obtained with adequate preparation, patience, repetition and perseverance.

Self-hypnosis or face-to-face hypnotherapy?

Whether the hypnotic trance state is arrived at through face-to-face hypnotherapy with a qualified practitioner or through self-hypnosis, the procedure is very similar. The main advantage of a face-to-face session is that a consultation process is gone through during which information is gathered so that the language used by the hypnotherapist during hypnosis is tailor-made to that of the listener. This increases the intensity of the therapy and the depth of the trance state, and can improve the success rate. However, as there are few registered hypnotherapists who also have first-hand knowledge of what a rider goes through when she has reached an all-time low on the confidence scale, self-hypnosis may be a more practical option.

A word of caution

I must stress that hypnotherapy is not a panacea for all ills. Certain conditions would make the therapy unsafe for the client, an example being where he or she suffers from schizophrenia or any type of psychotic personality disorder or psychosis already causing an altered state of mind. Furthermore, if you are receiving electroconvulsive therapy (ECT) or any form of treatment for a psychological problem, or if you suffer with low blood pressure, always check with your doctor before using hypnotherapy.

The conscious and unconscious mind

Hypnotherapy works by accessing the 'unconscious' mind as opposed to the 'conscious' mind, so what is meant by these terms? When we talk about the conscious mind, we refer to the thoughts that are going through our heads right now; the ones we are aware of as we think about something, the little voice on the shoulder, the one you can hear right now as you think of your shoulder. The conscious mind is rather less significant than our unconscious mind. To make it clearer, if you compare your mind to an iceberg (an analogy that one of my lecturers favoured), the tip you can see above the surface of the water is the conscious mind, and the larger, more substantial part out of sight below the water line (but supporting the tip), is the unconscious mind. So by comparison, the unconscious mind is somewhat larger.

The unconscious mind is the seat of our emotions and directs nearly all our behaviour. Everything that has ever happened to us, and everything we have ever seen, smelt, touched or heard is stored away there for future reference. It contains all our wisdom and intelligence; it is our source of creativity. The number of activities our unconscious mind performs and controls for us is quite astounding. Whenever we need to remember something (a name, date, place, an instruction, an understanding or insight), it pops out of our unconscious mind like magic, whether the conscious mind wants it to or not. We breathe, walk, talk, drive a car and use complicated pieces of technology, never giving a second thought as to where all that knowledge came from. But the conscious mind constantly takes credit for, and finds explanations for, the activities of the unconscious mind, over which it actually has no control and about which it is unaware.

Over the years, the conscious mind becomes very good at this act and it is able to offer such impressive rationalizations and explanations for its behaviour that we don't even question it. But the unconscious mind is

Changing your unconscious mind is the key to taking control of your fears.

much more observant, wise, intelligent, adaptive and skilful than the conscious mind could ever be. It is said that the conscious mind can only hold seven or eight thoughts at any one time, usually in reduced chunks, and this is why we tend to remember numbers more easily if they are in small bundles.

The nature of the conscious and unconscious minds

The unconscious mind can also delete information from our awareness. It would be impossible to process all the data we receive consciously, so the unconscious mind sorts it and then presents us with a summary of what is taking place. We have all heard anecdotal stories of extreme bravery in which someone had been badly injured yet felt no pain and had no awareness of his own injuries until after the traumatic event. In effect, the unconscious mind had sorted through the information and decided what the casualty needed to know to help his actions at that moment in time.

The interaction between the conscious and unconscious minds is happening all the time. Our conscious mind uses questions to reason and is always evaluating, both critically and analytically, by comparing and noticing. In hypnosis and the hypnotic trance state, however, it is dampened down and this allows excellent communication with the unconscious mind; and without its critical and analytical partner, changes in core beliefs and behaviours can take place. But this ability of the unconscious mind to accept without critical analysis has a downside because it can just as easily hang on to negative experiences. This means that whenever a similar event to one experienced previously recurs, your old feelings of discomfort are instantly brought back to the conscious mind in an attempt to protect you.

Wendy's story   A rider since 1977, Wendy suffered a serious accident, the result of which caused her to lose her confidence with horses. Her experience shows how past negative experiences can affect what we do in the present.

'Fourteen years ago I had an accident that put me in hospital with a trampled arm and severe concussion from two kicks to the head. This caused memory loss for three and half weeks and significant short-term memory loss for a further six. I had been asked to hack a horse for its owner, who "only used it for dressage" but wanted it exercised on days when she couldn't ride. The horse took off with me without warning, and eventually I became so unbalanced I toppled off underneath at speed. I gave up riding for four years after that, but then my children wanted lessons and I finally restarted.

'I bought my own horse in 2003 but although my accident had happened many years before, I found that the memory of it continued to affect my riding, causing me to be quite afraid and nervous at times. When I was at my worst with my nerves, I experienced various feelings of fear of being taken off with, fear of falling off, and specific fear of having the horse fall on top of me, breaking my pelvis. The physical symptoms I experienced could be a cold sweat, shaking, feeling sick, dramatic sudden whitening of pallor, dizziness. Latterly I began having full-blown panic attacks and agoraphobia to the point of being unable to go shopping as I would have to drive on an open stretch of moor to get to the supermarket.'

If you have had a bad experience on your horse, your unconscious mind may bring back all the negative thoughts, feelings and behaviours associated with that experience the next time you ride. This is very frustrating for the rider who knows rationally and logically that there is nothing actually happening in the present time to create these unwanted thoughts and feelings. It's a doubly hard pill to swallow when we aren't even sitting on the same horse any more!

What makes us feel nervous?

If you first of all accept that horse riding is a potentially dangerous activity, you are more than half way to understanding what's going on inside your mind and body when you ride. Nature has been very clever in installing a small chip in our brain, designed, amongst other things, to protect us if something life threatening is happening or is about to happen. This chip is known as the hypothalamus and is part of the endocrine system. Not surprisingly, when we do something it perceives as a potential threat, it starts to react and we then run into problems.

At this point the unconscious mind starts to ask questions such as:

What are you doing?
Why are you doing it?
Do you need to do it?
When will you stop doing it?
Do I need to take action?

At the same time, our conscious mind analyzes the situation from the stimuli it receives via our environment and our senses, and if the host – that's you and me – doesn't come up with a sensible, rational, logical and objective explanation, and the unconscious mind makes a connection between the outside stimuli and a previous negative experience, the chip in our brain starts to take charge. It then produces chemicals that will help the body to survive an attack; in other words, the fight-or-flight instinct that we horse riders hear so much about. When this happens, we feel the effects in all sorts of places such as our stomach, legs, arms, heart and head. Psychologically, it causes feelings of anxiety, stress, panic and fear. Phobias can be created, associated with this perceived threat, which can last for days, months or years. In severe cases it can cause depression, a less effective immune system and heart problems.

Fran's story   Fran is another rider of many years' standing. Her story illustrates how our unconscious mind can make the connection with outside stimuli and a previous negative experience, with undesirable consequences.

'I have been riding since I was four years old, with a gap from my early teens to late twenties. When I started to ride regularly again, I competed in horse trials, did a lot of cross country and hacked out extensively over all sorts of terrain. I have owned my present horse for three years, he is a 15.3 Hanoverian/Andalusian and has a very gentle and kind nature. I was able to fulfil my dream of becoming a horse owner when I emigrated to New Zealand in 1997.

'In 1987 I broke my neck in a riding accident but this did not deter me from riding, despite the negative attitude of my doctors. I am fortunate in that I did not lose the use of any limbs and, physically, I am fully recovered. Mentally, though, the whole experience was a shock. When I returned to riding after the accident I was not nervous, but I knew I had to be more careful about what I did. I became a mum in 1991 and noticed that before I even knew I was pregnant, something triggered caution within me – I suddenly didn't want to jump! I rode until five months into my pregnancy, when it became too uncomfortable and unbalancing. I found that after giving birth, I was much more cautious in my riding, aware that I now had the responsibility of another life. Some of the fun started to go out of it at this time.

'In 1996 I broke my right leg very badly in another riding accident. This was much worse than breaking my neck; it involved a long time in a wheelchair, a bone graft, metal plates and screws in my leg, and extensive and painful physiotherapy. During this time, we emigrated and I decided to give up riding. But there are so many wonderful horses in New Zealand I soon started again! This was when the nervousness became more apparent.

'The impact of nervousness on my riding shook my confidence as a person and led me to question my own worth. Riding had been such a huge part of my life for so long, and was also something I felt I had been good at. Some days I would shake and be weak at the knees before I even got on my horse. If he spooked, bucked or went a little faster than I wanted, I would get a sort of explosion of panic in my stomach, sometimes followed by a feeling of being

> Too much stress and anxiety can damage our health but small amounts keep us safe.

totally frozen up. I would hyperventilate and cry, and dismount as soon as I could. Sometimes, just the thought of riding would give me sleepless nights and stress. I would find any excuse not to ride – the weather, too much work, leg hurting, back hurting ... I would end a ride feeling frustrated, hating myself and utterly powerless to do anything about it.'

Effects of stress on the body

Stress and anxiety can have some rather devastating effects on the human body. When we are stressed, anxious or frightened, our brain releases adrenalin, noradrenalin and cortisol, chemicals synonymous with an 'alarm reaction' and part of the sympathetic nervous system.

As part of this alarm reaction:

- the eyes adjust to long vision in preparation for finding an escape route so that near vision becomes blurred
- the skin sweats and becomes pale as blood is drawn from the surface to important organs
- muscles under the skin partially contract in readiness to spring into action, causing 'goose pimples'
- the heart increases its output and blood pressure goes up so you feel your heart pounding
- breathing becomes more rapid so that adequate oxygen can be transferred to the blood
- the spleen releases more red blood cells from its store
- non-essential systems are inhibited so the digestive system slows and speech is difficult

With all this going on in the body, it's not surprising that:

- we feel sick and get headaches
- we feel hot or cold
- our muscles go into spasms and we shake
- we feel there is a knot in the stomach and we can't eat
- we are short of breath
- our mouths go dry and we can't get our words out
- our minds go blank and our concentration starts to deteriorate

Is this sounding familiar? If it's any consolation, at least you now know that you and your body will be prepared and will function perfectly normally should a sabre-toothed tiger suddenly appear in the middle of your dressage arena, pop up behind a show jump, or leap out from behind a bus shelter! Be assured, though: you are not alone, and hundreds like you experience this range of sensations every time they so much as even think about getting on their horses, let alone actually do it.

The fight-or-flight response

This fight-or-flight response theory is understandable and, as I've said, acceptable and very useful when faced with something that is actually life-threatening like that sabre-toothed tiger (I never actually came across one, by the way, but sometimes I'm sure my horse did!) – but when there is only a moderate danger or none at all, other than in our distorted perception, we need to be able to reduce the output of these chemicals and dampen down the psychological, emotional and behavioural responses they create.

Changing our perception of a situation, the way we think, changes the way we feel and alters the way we behave. But as our thoughts, feelings, behaviour and emotions are so closely entwined with one another, this sequence becomes more like an electrical circuit. When the circuit is activated anywhere along its length, it creates a chain reaction that completes the route before we even have time to consciously think about it. Which

> If we can stay in control
> of our emotions we can help our
> horses to do the same.

comes first is still debated in the medical field; some feel that the chemical response is activated by the mere thought of danger or by acting as if frightened, while others feel the unconscious, instinctive part of our brain picks up signals we are not aware of and then produces the chemicals. All we really need to concern ourselves with is the question, how do we break this cycle, short-circuit it, and change the negative direction in which the electrical current is flowing to a positive one? This is where hypnotherapy, hypnosis and the hypnotic trance state start to work.

Of course, there is an additional problem in this equation, which the horse rider has to deal with. While this situation of a fight-or-flight response will normally only affect our own physiological well-being, when there is a second party involved in this scenario, you can see that there are going to be even more undesirable consequences as a result of how we are thinking, feeling and behaving in any given situation, especially when that second party is a creature that lives and survives by its own acute sense of its environment. Because we will be sending out signals like a satellite dish, this sensitive creature is going to be picking up and tuning in to every channel we broadcast. And the name of this beast? None other than the animal on which we lavish so much time and attention yet don't feel brave or confident enough to enjoy the experience when we sit on its back, the horse!

case study

Louise's story

A series of falls left Louise feeling fearful when riding and her experience demonstrates just how easy it is to pass negative feelings to the horse.

'My first pony was killed in a road accident after I fell off him. When I first owned Kate, my second horse, I had her professionally broken but she was still very spooky. I fell off her and she cantered across my back and terrorized the village for three hours before anyone could catch her. I took her to a livery yard to be re-broken, and to get my confidence back. I had loads of lessons on the school horse while my instructor took Kate right back to basics. Eventually, we appeared to have overcome our problems and I took her home. A year later, my friend and I were out hacking and a loud noise caused both horses to spook; I came off over Kate's shoulder and landed on my head. I suffered a compression fracture in one of my vertebrae, and was out of action for five months.

'Captain, a ten-year-old ex-hunter followed and I fell off him in the school while jumping, dislocating my elbow. My last fall was in September 2000. As a result of this, I became very cautious in my riding. On a hack, I'd get to a certain point and just feel physically weak and unable to go on. If Captain spooked I would leave the situation mentally; the best way I can describe it is that my mind would simply go to white noise, similar to when the aerial plug is pulled out of the back of a television. Understandably, Captain would realize he was on his own and spook even more! When I saw other people on the yard go out on their horses and then come back some time later, safe and sound, I would feel angry with myself for not being able to do the same. I felt stupid because I couldn't bring myself to do something that everyone else took for granted, on much scarier horses! I would ride out on Captain with someone from the yard on a school horse and when Captain spooked or jogged, I would just get off and swap horses. Sometimes, I'd cry when I got home and I'm sure my partner wondered why I kept on riding; it certainly didn't seem to be making me happy.'

What we have to understand as riders is that not only do we need to conquer our fears, anxieties and lack of confidence for our own benefit, but we also need to overcome them for the benefit of the horse. If we don't, we run into the problem of the rider actually creating the very situation she is trying to avoid: a nervous horse which then makes a nervous rider, which makes a more nervous horse and an even more nervous rider...

The aim of hypnotherapy for the rider

During the state of hypnosis, when the conscious mind is bypassed and the unconscious part of the mind is spoken to, if we stay with the electrical metaphor, the negative current is short-circuited, reversed in a positive direction, and rejoined to a positive terminal. Once we have reprogrammed the unconscious mind and it reconnects with the conscious mind, our perception alters. We feel different and, depending on the reason for hypnotherapy, we find that whatever blockage was stopping us from achieving our goal has either been reduced to such a degree that we can now live with it, or it has been removed completely.

case study

Tessa's story In common with the other riders who have shared their stories with us, Tessa tried hypnotherapy as a way of helping her overcome her fears with horses.

'I started riding as a child and returned to it again in 1994. A few falls didn't help the nerves at all but I desperately wanted to ride, so I kept at it. At the end of 1998 I spent a weekend at Richard Maxwell's yard and it inspired me to take a horse on loan the following year. I had BJ for eighteen months and despite living through periods of naked terror with him, finally managed to hack out on my own. I have a particular fear of what the horse will do in open spaces, having been bolted with on several occasions. I also didn't like the fear of the unknown, and would bail out or get off at the slightest excuse.

'My present horse is called Yogi and he was purchased with the idea of doing a little dressage. So far we have managed some in-hand classes at our local show, which is actually quite a serious one. Yogi and I were told off very gently by the judge for "not acting our age" but I was just happy to make it into the arena at all!

'I had heard that self-hypnosis could be very effective in helping to deal with fear, and because I had become quite desperate and very depressed about the whole situation with my horse, I decided to give it a go. It took about a week before I noticed any changes, and although I would not say I have improved in confidence as such, I feel so much better now I know that I can control the panics to a certain extent.

'The biggest improvement is in dear sweet Yogi, who has become positively brave. Today he was perfect; facing a stiff breeze, model aircraft and Shetland ponies – all of which would have terrified him in the past and made him impossible to ride for at least a day. But today he stood perfectly still when I mounted and immediately began to seek a contact as we moved off. He has also passed fireworks – he doesn't like them particularly but he concentrates on me not being scared.

'I find I experience relapses from time to time but they are definitely getting fewer. Yogi used to be able to spark them off by getting 'lit up' and upset. But as I get calmer, so does he. Thanks to self-hypnosis, I can see a future with my horse now, where at one point it seemed impossible. We will just keep going even if we never make it to the top. If we ever do, it will be the icing on the cake of my friendship with my horse.'

The hypnotic process

Before I describe the various stages of hypnosis, I want to lay to rest any misconceptions that you may have about the power of hypnotherapy and the hypnotic trance state. Despite impressions given in the media and by those who 'perform' hypnosis for entertainment, hypnotherapy cannot make you do anything, say anything or behave in any way that is unnatural to you. It cannot override your sense of morality, alter your judgement about what is right and wrong, or make you more susceptible to the unethical behaviours of others. During a hypnotic trance you will always be aware of your surroundings when you need to be; you will still hear a fire alarm go off, be able to open your eyes, and get up hold the thought

> Hypnosis allows you to search inside
> your mind and discover how much
> control you really have.

and walk away, for example. You will always be in control, just as you are in a fully wakeful state. A hypnotic trance state is arrived at by 'agreement', not by way of coercion.

The induction sequence

During hypnosis you are taken on a journey through increasingly deeper stages, beginning with the induction of the trance state, a day-dreamy state of mind, similar to that experienced while listening to music or driving for a long time on a boring stretch of road, or listening to a long lecture or during meditation. Think how many times you have driven home from somewhere but can't remember the actual journey, or while in the middle of listening to someone speaking, you have drifted off to somewhere else. It is that half-awake feeling as you drift to the surface of sleep, caught between it and wakefulness. These are trance states or altered states of mind.

This induction sequence allows your body and mind to move into a stage of complete relaxation, preparing them to transfer to the next stage of the hypnotic process. Breathing techniques, relaxation, visualization imagery, the use of figurative or descriptive language, or bombarding the critical mind with an overload of information can all induce the mind to start to alter its state of awareness. The old stereotypical image of swinging a watch in front of a subject's eyes is to some extent valid as another technique to get the conscious critical mind to switch off. Today there are all sorts of hi-tech gadgets and gimmicks available that create moving shapes or noises but they are just that – gimmicks.

When it comes to listening to self-hypnosis CDs, there is no concrete evidence to suggest that using music, two different voices in stereo sound or special sound effects actually increase the success of the process at all. Clients of mine who have tried these techniques elsewhere have told me that they actually found them most annoying and, rather than allowing them to focus on the voice, they actually distracted them to such an extent that they gave up using the process. Why re-invent the wheel if it works as it is?

The trigger

The next stage of the hypnotic process is called the trigger. Depending on the therapeutic training of the hypnotherapist and her personal preference, different techniques will be used to increase the depth of the trance state. Sometimes a word or a particular behaviour is offered, such as touching one's ear or pressing a finger and thumb together. This trigger can be used in the normal waking state to reproduce the same state of calmness and relaxation achieved during hypnosis. It can also be used to bring back to the conscious mind any imagery or suggestion that the unconscious mind has visualized or heard during therapy. It is always emphasized by the hypnotherapist that this trigger word or action will only take on its special meaning when used in relation to hypnosis at that time. In all other circumstances the word or action will have the same meaning as it always had.

The deepener

The third level of the process is called the deepener, where the mind is taken through a process that encourages the critical conscious mind to fade into the background and the unconscious mind to come forward, enabling a much deeper hypnotic trance state to be established. This state is associated with a vivid involvement in imagined events, a shift into a context-free, literal understanding of words and phrases, and a removal of the restrictions ordinarily imposed upon conscious abilities and responses. Hypnotherapy is designed to take full advantage of these characteristics. The trigger and deepener stages are interwoven with each other and during them the listener is taken ever further from the conscious world.

A deep trance state will be easier to attain with practice but trying too hard will prevent it.

The therapeutic stage

The hypnotic trance state then progresses to the therapeutic stage. At this stage the critical conscious mind can be bypassed completely, and the unconscious mind is ready to absorb new information; in other words the negative electric current can now be short circuited, overridden and then rejoined to positive terminals. While the unconscious mind is in this receptive state, the therapist will talk directly to it, offering suggestions and ideas, but above all, directly addressing the issue that is concerning the listener most. The language spoken by the therapist at this stage is more precise, and often quite directive. The listener will be able to access imagined events clearly and calmly, to such an extent that it is possible for her to undergo the same changes in her beliefs that she would have experienced had the situation been real. During this stage new ways of thinking are established and laid down for future recall, and as long as these ideas, concepts, instructions or behaviours do not conflict with the listener's own moral beliefs, these will remain with her when she returns to a fully wakeful state.

Once the unconscious mind is reprogrammed, it can positively influence the conscious mind in any given situation or any series of events. Our perceptions of the situation can be altered; we may feel differently about it, perhaps more relaxed, calmer, optimistic, energized, healthier, motivated and more in control of our responses, habits and behaviours. This control increases our confidence. With growing confidence comes the realization that we can actually achieve those goals we never thought possible and the actual subsequent achievement is our biofeedback. But hypnosis can go further than this; we can actually change the way our body functions.

All through a hypnotherapy session, whether it be face-to-face with a therapist or listening to a self-hypnosis CD, positive language is used to encourage, motivate and reward your achievements. Confidence building is the foundation block of the whole process, and added to this are other more specific elements. Interwoven within the language used are suggestions, concepts and ideas that will help you long after the session has finished. You will experience the actual event or events you are struggling to deal with, but this time you will only experience positive sensations. You will see the goal you want and actually be there. You will use all your senses to experience this achievement, feeling all the positive emotions associated with it. All negative non-productive thoughts, concepts, ideas, feelings and behaviours are reduced or rationalized and put into their true perspectives. Post-hypnotic anchors (physical or mental reminders that are used to help you recall the positive sensations, feelings, emotions and ideas after the trance has ended) are used to enable you to make an instant connection between the thoughts, feelings and emotions that you have experienced during the hypnotic state to the here-and-now situation you are in.

The termination

The final stage, the termination, is when the hypnotic trance is brought to an end and you are gently returned to full consciousness and wakefulness. During this process you are offered the option of bringing back into your conscious world all the thoughts, feelings and behaviours you have experienced during the hypnotic trance, and leaving behind any you do not want. This suggestion allows you to decide for yourself what you have found most pleasurable and beneficial, and what you may wish to hold in your conscious mind.

Often during hypnosis, you may experience various physiological and biological changes. For example:

- your arms and legs may feel either particularly heavy or so light they could be floating
- you may experience a tingling sensation in them or feel as if they are not there any more

After hypnotherapy, changes may be sudden and dramatic or slow and gradual, almost going unnoticed.

- you may be aware of your heartbeat slowing and your breathing becoming shallower
- sometimes the stomach can start to bubble and gurgle
- your eyes may water more than usual and your eyelids flutter
- you may feel reluctant to move and that there has been a distortion in the passing of time
- as you start to drift back from the hypnotic state you may experience a feeling of euphoria and well-being

When the session is finished, you should be left feeling very calm, relaxed and peaceful although the positive feelings of motivation and confidence can often take some time to develop. There doesn't seem to be any particular reason why hypnotherapy works instantly for some people, but takes time for others. Even when it feels as though nothing at all has actually happened, you will be surprised at just how much actually has changed. This may only be noticed in retrospect as you look back at how you were before you started using hypnosis.

case study

Louise's story continues   Earlier in the chapter Louise recalled her experiences of fear. In tackling her problem she decided to try self-hypnosis and this is her account of the trance state.

'Hypnotic trances varied quite a lot for me. Sometimes I really wouldn't know anything about it until the countdown at the end, at other times my legs just wouldn't behave themselves and would be aching and feeling heavy. Most times, though, the trance would feel like the sensation you have just before you fall asleep; when you're not actually asleep and not fully awake.'

Self-hypnosis

As I have mentioned before, the hypnotic trance state through self-hypnosis is the same as through face-to-face therapy, and CDs are a more cost-effective and convenient option. Once you have found a title that fits your problem, you can listen to that one as often as you like. You can listen to more than one CD, for different problem areas as long as you leave 12 hours between them. If you decide to try a self-hypnosis CD, the following tips may be helpful.

- Find a quiet room where you know you won't be disturbed.
- Dim the lights or turn them off.
- You may choose to light a candle or use scented oils.
- Make sure you are comfortable before you start, on a soft chair that supports the head or lying on a couch or bed.
- Don't jump up straightaway after the CD ends – give yourself some time to be peaceful

Research shows that audio CDs are most effective when listened to daily for the first week and as often as possible thereafter, and especially before an event that may have caused apprehension in the past.

Don't worry if you feel you have slept while listening to the CD; the sub-conscious mind is capable of absorbing positive suggestions even in a light sleep state. If you find that you sleep on past the ending of the CD, however, then your sleep state has been too deep. In this case, listen to it in a less sleep-inducing environment, maybe in a more upright position or with the lights on, for example. Don't listen to it when you are tired at the end of the day or in need of sleep.

WARNING!

Do not listen to the CD while driving, operating machinery, or taking part in any activity that requires your full and undivided concentration.

If you suffer with low blood pressure that requires medication, consult your doctor before using hypnotherapy. This is because the heart rate often slows down during hypnosis due to the deep state of relaxation.

> If you sleep past the end of your self-hypnosis CD, change your resting position next time.

Remember that, exactly as in a face-to-face session, you will always be in control and able to override the trance while listening to a self-hypnosis CD. If anything should need your attention, you will be able to open your eyes as normal and deal with any situation. You will always be in control of your own actions at all times, and the content of the CD cannot make you do anything you would not normally do. It will, however, help to encourage you to overcome, and take control of those fears, worries, anxieties and negative thoughts that are preventing you from achieving your full potential.

case study

Alison's story

Alison was delighted with her new horse but fear blocked her enjoyment of him. Here she explains how the use of a self-hypnosis CD helped her overcome the obstacle.

'Last spring I took a rising four-year-old Appaloosa called Dylan on a four-week trial, with a view to buying him. I originally had no intention of buying a youngster, as my last horse had reached the grand old age of twenty-seven and, although prone to the odd outburst, was a very reliable and confidence-inspiring hack. However, having tried and rejected umpteen mature horses and had some pretty scary experiences – including being run away with twice! – I thought I'd give Dylan a try, since a blank canvas had begun to seem like a much more attractive prospect than an older horse with built-in hang-ups.

'Dylan had just been backed and I began riding him out with a very experienced friend on foot, and all went well. By the end of the trial period I was well and truly smitten with his gentle, comical character and he hadn't put a foot wrong while out quietly riding round the lanes where we live. Once ownership had passed to me, however, I was struck by the heavy responsibility that I now had. I began to feel that I was going to wreck this lovely horse because my riding wasn't good enough, and I was going to turn him into a timid bundle of nerves by not showing enough confidence myself. This became a bit of a self-fulfilling prophecy and every ride seemed more daunting than the last. I became really pretty scared.

'Throughout all this, Dylan strolled calmly round the lanes, showing great interest in the new green shoots in the hedges, developing a mild dislike of manhole covers, never running away, never seriously napping, just being a really normal, genuine, young horse. Even so, I found that it didn't matter how well behaved he was, I still had an image in my mind of how bad things could be, and that was enough to make me nervous. I wasn't going to give up, though.

'I had the help of a confident expert friend, and a really forgiving horse. I did two things: I kept regular entries in my "Dylan Diary", and referred back to them when I felt really low. I was surprised by how many great rides I'd had where everything had been fine and I'd felt OK. I also bought and listened to a confidence-building audio CD that I had seen recommended on the Internet. I listened to the whole recording twice over a couple of days and enjoyed how relaxing it was, but I honestly didn't feel as if it was changing my response to riding. However, on my first hack I realized that I wasn't nearly as anxious as I had been before. I found that being able to relax completely while listening to the CD had given me room to be rational about my riding experiences, and I could tap into that calm while I was in the saddle. It really worked for me and by the end of the summer Dylan and I had our first canter together and I was absolutely thrilled! (Dylan seemed pretty chuffed with himself too!)'

hold the thought

If you can relax completely while listening to the CD, you can 'tap' into that calm while in the saddle.

Reasons why hypnosis fails

As I explained earlier, those people who are very analytical and question everything to such an extent that they find it impossible to accept a concept they perhaps don't fully understand, may find the trance state eludes them. If you find losing control or enjoying yourself doesn't come easily, this can also make relaxing into a hypnotic state very difficult.

Sometimes hypnosis fails because we self-sabotage the process, and I know this sounds odd when you really are convinced in your own mind that you want something to change, but just imagine this scenario. Let's say you have convinced those around you that if you had your own horse, you really would have everything you ever desired. And although it will mean a financial struggle, others support your quest. After a long search, involving many miles of travelling and at great expense, both financially and in time, you find your horse. But you then find that owning a horse is not quite what you expected it to be; you don't like all the time and work involved, so you just turn the horse out. You are disappointed, but feel reluctant to admit this even to yourself. Everyone tells you how lucky you are to have a horse and what a perfect find he is, but this puts even more pressure on you, setting up an internal mental conflict. If this conflict is not dealt with, physical symptoms can appear. The mind will try to do whatever it can to relieve this stress and often a phobia or fear can start. Now the mind has created a justifiable, logical reason for avoiding a situation; 'I don't ride my horse now because I am frightened to', and this is acceptable not only to you the rider, but also to others.

Removing the phobia or fear would mean that the rider would have to a: admit she had made a mistake and face the consequences, and b: perhaps sell the horse. This may be worse than actually having the phobia or fear.

Perhaps you avoid competitions because, deep down, you are not very competitive, even though others feel you should be. Perhaps a partner or parents are pressurizing you to justify the expense of your hobby if you don't compete, and it's easier to say you are fearful than you really aren't interested. Or perhaps you are more worried about failure, of not living up to others' expectations, so avoiding the situation altogether is a safer alternative.

Another blockage to this process could be that the issues around riding are only a reflection of what is going on elsewhere in your life. If you are a nervous, anxious person generally, and you find situations at work, home or socially provoke similar feelings of panic, nervousness and fear, then it's a lot to expect that in this one area of life, riding, you are suddenly going to become a very confident, self-assured and relaxed person. It may be that if you seek help in getting to the root of the problem with regard to other issues in your life, the horse-related ones will lessen, if not disappear altogether.

For those who have found hypnosis to work, it has sometimes been a real lifesaver, a last clutch of a straw before throwing the grooming brush to the floor and hanging up the boots.

case study

Fran's story concludes

Wendy and Fran earlier shared their experiences of how their loss of confidence spoiled their involvement with their horses. Happily, like Louise, Alison and Tessa, their stories don't end there as each rider tackled her problem through self-hypnosis to great effect. Fran ends ...

'Before I tried self-hypnosis to help me with my problem, I tried relaxation and positive thinking. I tried Rescue Remedy, I tried letting go of the things that scared me most (jumping and hacking out) and concentrated on dressage. I attempted to take the positive things from each ride and let go of the negative ones. I constantly punished myself and tried to "just get over it". These things helped sometimes, but I still could not conquer the demon that seemed to be firmly lodged inside me.

'I bought a self-hypnosis CD but, not knowing anything about the therapy beforehand, I was initially concerned about trying it because I worried it would trigger unwanted emotions, or even make me a little crazy! However, even though I was apprehensive the first time, it was a very pleasant experience. Each time I used the CD I found it easier to let go and relax, and it was wonderful to set aside that hour just for me! I listened to the disc every evening for the first week, missed a few evenings the second, and every evening the third as this was "pre-show" week, so I needed reinforcement!

Don't be afraid to talk.
Counselling may help.

'I rode the day after I listened to the CD for the first time and found an immediate improvement. I was still a bit nervous but could "ride through" the nerves, using the relaxation word. My breathing improved and my horse also improved! In my weekly lesson, three days afterwards, my instructor noticed a huge difference – I was riding my horse forward and with confidence, and was much more relaxed. I let her into my "secret" (I had told no one but my family) and she embraced the idea wholeheartedly. The next day I rode my horse in the paddock (another "big deal" for me) and actually jumped him.

'My confidence continued to build; in the following week's lesson we even went in the cross-country paddock and galloped up the hill! When Maze put in an exuberant buck, I just laughed and rode him on. A month previously that would have meant a panic attack, dismounting and taking several weeks to regain any sort of confidence. By the third week, we'd coped with a very windy, spooky day with Maze doing his patented "stop and spin", and I was happily riding him home to his paddock in just a halter.

'While I was in a hypnotic trance I felt very relaxed, calm, safe and comfortable. The first time I cried a little at the "this is how it was always meant to be" part, but soon became comfortable and positive with this. After the session finished, I still felt relaxed and calm, but alert and centred. My body felt more balanced and I think it has helped my long-standing back problems too.

'I would recommend this form of self-help therapy to anyone, and I have! If it can help me, it can help anyone, as long as they really want to continue riding. Using self-hypnosis has restored to me one of the greatest pleasures in my life. I am able to make short and long-term goals for my riding, rather than struggling each day with the nervousness that blocked any potential I, or my horse, had. Maze is also responding very well to having a rider who is more fun and can give him confidence too. Nervousness no longer has the power to affect my whole life or restrict the things I do when riding. I feel I have recovered the "rider within", the one who has been buried for so long.'

Taking control

You can see from the case studies and stories included in this chapter that people from all walks of life come to horses and riding. Sometimes it's the realization of a childhood dream, sometimes the rekindling of a long-lost hobby, or the interest arrives by accident, often through 'cross-contamination' – the idea of 'if you can't beat them, you might as well join them' – but we all have different stories to tell relating to our fears and anxieties, and how they have affected our lives as riders.

The fascination we have with the horse is so embedded and entrenched in our psyche that it is often hard to explain to someone who has never been bitten by this bug why we are often prepared to put ourselves through so much pain, anguish and discomfort to achieve our goals. Giving up riding altogether is often not a perceived option. In an attempt to hang on to a way of life we feel lovingly entrapped by, we will continue to keep our beloved four-legged friends as companions, acknowledging inwardly that we sometimes feel helpless, frustrated with ourselves, and desperate. We live in the hope that one day, the feelings of fear and dread that prevent us from riding with confidence will somehow have disappeared from our minds while we slept through the night.

Each day we hope that, for some reason, something has changed, perhaps because the sun is shining, the wind has died down, the road works have finished, the litter has all been collected or that blooming dog is indoors. Maybe the jumps are more inviting, the approach more controlled, or the poles are more solid. Perhaps even, the dressage judge has missed that spook, you manage to remember to breathe, or the horse strikes off on the right leg; better still, the horse has read the dressage test beforehand.

There may be any wishful number of reasons as to why today may be different from all the others, but unfortunately, it rarely is. So the next time your negative thoughts – those automatic ones that jump into your mind

> Don't set yourself up to fail.
> Take one step at a time.

before you have a chance to challenge them – stop you in your tracks, remember: you do have an option. You can change those thoughts, you can change those feelings and you can change the behaviours they create. You may not become the next John Whittaker, Carl Hester or Pippa Funnell, but you may enjoy the delights of hacking down a country lane or a main road, popping over a clear round course or a fallen log, or doing an unaffiliated dressage test. For many of us, this is as big an accomplishment as receiving an Olympic gold medal, *and it is achievable.*

case study

Wendy's story ends

'When I was at the worst with my nerves, I tried having riding lessons every single day for six months to expose myself to my fears. This seemed to be a good plan of action, but although I developed excellent balance, the lessons simply didn't help me to overcome the nervousness I was battling with. In desperation I then had two sessions with a hypnotherapist, which did make a difference; but I still felt that I needed some sort of back-up.

'Having used a self-hypnosis book some years ago to help me cope with stress, I decided to try the therapy again, this time using a CD. I found the experience to be very relaxing and so was encouraged to persevere with it. I generally used it at night before I went to sleep. I tended to wake up as the CD ended and then I fell deeply asleep very quickly. I used to be a restless sleeper, but found that I slept through without interruption after I had used the CD.

'In addition to helping me sleep better, I noticed that I felt calmer within myself as a result of self-hypnosis. I also believe I am now a much happier person.

'I didn't ride until I had listened to the CD twice, but *everybody* noticed the difference in my riding immediately. I have recommended the therapy to several members of my riding club because the results I have had are nothing short of miraculous. People just could not believe the change in me they were seeing in front of their very eyes! I was apparently a technically good rider, but the tension I used to feel made the experience of riding miserable and inhibited. After I'd had my hypnotherapy sessions with a therapist, it was pointed out to me that I did in fact look less tense, but it wasn't until I had used a *Confident Rider* self-hypnosis CD that real changes began to happen. My instructors and a dressage judge all enthused about how relaxed I was and how much I was getting out of my horse as a result. I found myself really looking forward to my daily lessons and not taking any notice of the spooking that used to bother me so much. Out hacking on my own horse, which had been a major issue before, I actually found myself laughing out loud when she spooked in an open field at a pheasant that flew up in front of her nose. At one time I would have been off her in a flash, just in case she took off.

'Looking back, I can say that I was an extremely nervous rider, and my nerves, and my inability to control them robbed me of many of life's pleasures. Self-hypnosis has certainly helped me to conquer my fears and I would recommend it to any rider lacking in confidence.'

5

The NLP Approach to Confident Riding

Liz Morrison

'NLP sports psychology offers an understanding
of why you are experiencing fear and, more
importantly, a way of changing your attitude
to help you overcome it.'

The NLP approach

In this section I will be exploring how
the Neuro-Linguistic Programming (NLP)
approach to sports psychology can help you
to develop confidence when riding. Because of
how the horse relates to us, many people, especially women, find that
improved confidence in their riding actually has a knock-on effect in
different areas of their lives too. NLP is a way of teaching the mind to have
more choices about how to respond to a situation, rather than letting
habitual responses and attitudes, such as fear or self-doubt, get in the way.

The section highlights that accepting fear and overcoming it through
horses can be a part of a journey to increased self-confidence in all areas of
your life. Simply understanding that fear is a normal response, which is
triggered by what you believe and the previous experiences you have had,
helps you to begin to change. Examples from my clients and their stories are
used to demonstrate different aspects of this work. Each needed a slightly
different solution in order to progress, and these are explained to help
demonstrate the tools of the NLP sports psychology approach.

As you will read, for each person an increased degree of self-knowledge
was very important. They needed to recognize not only where their current
performance was at, but also the beliefs and repetitious behaviours that were
keeping it in that limiting place. Through their stories you can build up a
picture of the different exercises and activities that you could use in your
own situation.

For many people it is helpful to realize that there are others just like them,
sharing the same fears and drops in performance. As you read you imagine
you are going through the same experiences as the people in the case
studies. If they can move forward, then so can you! NLP can help you make
lasting changes to your relationship with horses, and with it, the opportunity
to achieve more in other aspects of your life, too.

Many people find that improved confidence in riding has a knock-on effect on the rest of their lives.

case study

People like you

Christina is a mum in her early thirties who used to compete at affiliated level. After a break to have a couple of kids she was delighted to buy a young horse on which to get going again then found she had lost her confidence and felt she was simply deteriorating as a rider. She couldn't explain why riding was so important to her, but not being able to ride as well as she had was certainly affecting her life. This caused tension at home as the cost of keeping the horse and coping with two small children took its toll.

Stephen is a young professional rider who wanted to take exams and compete but was effectively paralyzed with fears about whether he was good enough and what people would think when they watched him. As a result his performance became very variable, and his supporters were beginning to take away the horses they had given him to compete.

Joanne had had an accident out hacking, when her horse spooked and caused a car to crash. Although nobody was seriously injured, she began to have flashbacks, panic attacks and confidence crises, not just out hacking but also in an increasing range of riding situations. She felt unable to ride out of the arena and was beginning to simply put off riding her horse.

I have chosen these case studies because they illustrate how fear and loss of confidence can creep in, in so many different ways. They also illustrate the range of techniques that can be applied to rebuild confidence. Full explanations about the actual techniques that are used, and more detail about NLP sports psychology for riders can be found in my book *Simple Steps to Riding Success* and on the website: www.positiveriding.co.uk.

Accepting fear

Susan Jeffers, the renowned American psychologist and author, suggests that fear will always be present if we are growing and developing as human beings.

In her opinion, the trick is not to avoid feeling it, but rather to accept it and work with it. Meeting your fear and overcoming it is a powerful and resourceful experience with which to approach the next issue that life presents. Alois Podhajsky, a famous director of the Spanish Riding School, made a lovely statement that shows how this line of thinking is relevant even at the most professional level: '... I must not forget to thank the difficult horses who made my life miserable, but who were better teachers than the well behaved school horses who raised no problems.'

We have all admired great horsemen and women who can transform horses and perform in a relaxed and positive style around them. Yet sometimes we do not fully appreciate how much horses can transform humans! They are such engrossing and challenging partners that it is difficult to be involved with a horse and not be touched in significant ways. For those seeking personal growth, horses can therefore be a very effective catalyst that helps us to become less fearful, more powerful, more in touch with our real selves.

The fact that we so consistently seek out horses is testimony to their magnetic power and the strength of our desire for mastery over our fears. Perhaps one of the gifts a horse offers is a chance to explore constructive ways to meet danger and manage our private fears. Horses can give us confidence in our own innate resourcefulness, reminding us that we have the ability, intuition and flexibility to pass through challenging events.

Often a rider experiencing nervousness or lack of confidence when riding will behave with low self-esteem in other areas of their life too. Conversely, sometimes riders who come to me with confidence problems are confused at why they have this issue when they are so confident or strong in the rest of their life. Often they have a core insecurity, hidden at work or home, which

> Horses are so engrossing. It is difficult to be involved with them and not be touched in significant ways.

is brought out in their relationship with the horse. After all, it is hard to sit on an animal weighing one thousand pounds and not be aware of its power! So riding and the relationship with the horse can bring deeply hidden issues to the surface, acting as a magnifying glass or mirror to your responses.

Understanding yourself

It is useful to realize that whenever you confront a fear and overcome it by whatever approach, you will become more confident about facing a similar situation the next time. As Mary Midkiff, the author of She Flies Without Wings explains: 'Whether our "jumps" come on a cross-country course or within our workplaces and homes ... we gain confidence every time we soar over them. Danger and our mastery of it become moments that make us more capable of handling the next danger and facing other risks.'

Now, let's be realistic: people can and do get hurt handling and riding horses. The ultimate conundrum for riders is that the more you are 'afraid', the more the horse will behave in a way that frightens you. And tension in the rider comes in many forms. Whether it is a fear of falling off, a fear of a accident happening to you while riding out, or the more subtle fear of being judged or making mistakes in front of people who matter to you, the horse will pick it up. NLP sports psychology offers an understanding of why you are experiencing fear, and, more importantly, a way of changing your attitude to help you overcome it.

However, one point I would like to reinforce is that *we* choose to ride the horse; it does not get much chance to choose who rides it! The rider is therefore responsible for the interaction with the horse – the horse does not intend to give you a bad ride or ruin your self-confidence. I would like to suggest that you have a responsibility to continually improve your riding in order to be able to relate better and better to the horse.

For many people, one of the classic dilemmas brought out by riding for many people is the need to be in control, often driven by a need for security. Yet paradoxically the control needed is not that of the horse, but of yourself, and your ability to manage your emotional state. Are you enough in control to be able to relax and let go, and so access all your unconscious abilities?

As an instructor, I hear of many people who say they want to work as a partner with their horses but are fearful and so use strong bits, martingales, nosebands – then drive it forwards with spurs and whips. They start out a little afraid of the horse, and the horse, detecting this, begins to behave 'badly' – spooking, head up, jogging and so on. Remember that the horse is not being bad – that is our judgement – he is just responding defensively to how he is being ridden. Add in a consideration of the rider's balance, saddle fitting and other causes of pain and discomfort, and there are many reasons why a horse will behave defensively.

The cycle seems pretty obvious, and it is useful to realize the horse will have had past experiences that also determine how it reacts. When a horse's confidence is undermined, for instance if it has had a difficult past, it is less likely to be able to help someone with a fear of riding.

Sometimes the emphasis is on teaching more advanced movements rather than on a deeper understanding of the horse. It is important to realize that not all teachers are able to address the source of confidence problems. Some may even endorse increasing the severity of the tack in proportion to the fear and lack of competence. If you believe you can control danger with external devices, be aware that they will in fact heighten the tension and fear felt by both horse and rider. As well as getting correct technical riding instruction, you need to find your own inner courage and learn to relax on a horse.

> The control needed is not that of
> the horse, but of yourself, and
> your ability to manage your
> emotional state.

From my experience, understanding values and beliefs is one of the most valuable starting points for helping people build their confidence and self-esteem. This is because they drive our behaviour and help us understand who we are. When they are all aligned and working together you will have a well-balanced and motivated state of mind. When they are in conflict there will be a sense of disjointedness and disharmony, where self-belief is weakened. This is often the state that leads to fear.

Finding out what you value is a relatively simple exercise, although it does need a certain amount of careful thought. It revolves round asking a simple but specific question: '*Why* is that important to you?' Stephen's case study illustrates how the process works.

Stephen's story   I started by asking Stephen, 'Why do you like eventing?' His answers, as you can see opposite, included:

- it involves skill across three disciplines
- it's fun
- it's incredible to share such a test with a horse
- it's the ultimate test

For each of these answers, and the others he gave, I kept asking the same core question until we had another layer of answers, then another. I wrote down his answers so that he could keep track of what I was doing, starting at the bottom of a piece of paper. At first this seemed like quite an odd process, he thought I was missing the point. This was not about goal setting or visualization! And the answers seemed so obvious to him: surely everyone thought the way he did? Still, he humoured me.

He watched the answers mapping out in front of him like a tree; branches came out from the start point, then twigs and leaves. Other people describe this process like peeling back the layers of an onion. Stephen's four original answers branched out to become the diagram on the opposite page. The arrows indicate where the 'Why is that important?' question was asked. Where two or more answers stemmed from the question, they have been followed to their conclusion before returning to the answer.

There were obviously some repeating themes emerging from Stephen's answers. The ones at the end of the branches tend to be values and beliefs so for Stephen these are along the themes of:

- keep improving
- life is for living
- have choice
- be respected
- be successful

We will return to the significance of these for Stephen shortly.

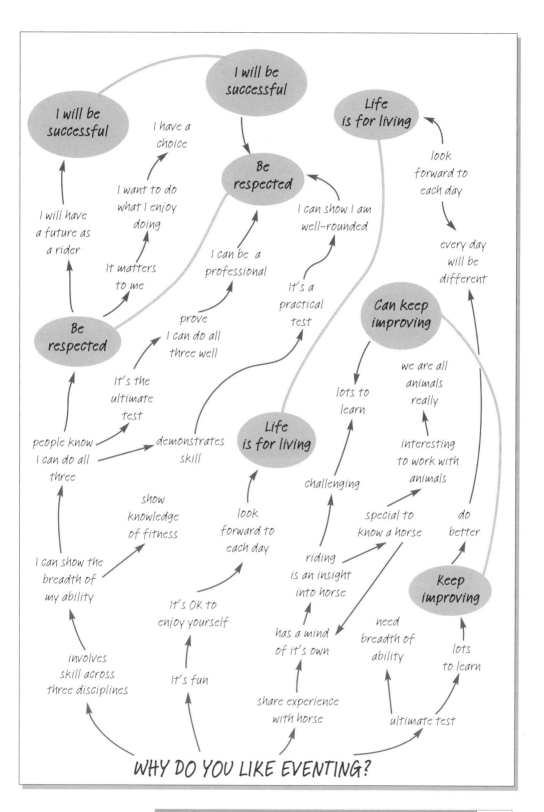

I will be successful

I will be successful

Life is for living

I have a choice

I want to do what I enjoy doing

Be respected

I can show I am well-rounded

look forward to each day

I will have a future as a rider

It matters to me

I can be a professional

It's a practical test

every day will be different

Be respected

prove I can do all three well

Can keep improving

lots to learn

we are all animals really

It's the ultimate test

demonstrates skill

Life is for living

interesting to work with animals

people know I can do all three

show knowledge of fitness

look forward to each day

challenging

special to know a horse

do better

I can show the breadth of my ability

It's OK to enjoy yourself

riding is an insight into horse

Keep improving

involves skill across three disciplines

It's fun

has a mind of it's own

need breadth of ability

lots to learn

share experience with horse

ultimate test

WHY DO YOU LIKE EVENTING?

The power of belief

From my work with riders I have found that there are four main reasons for wanting to relate with horses. Some of these are clearly connected to values; for example, connecting to nature, learning, an appreciation of beauty and art, while others use the horse as a means to an end – in particular meeting a need to be in control and proving they are good, gaining respect and similar themes. Other values people hold include security, connecting with others, a sense of community and family relationships. Once you understand just what is motivating you, it is easy to recognize why little incidents can affect your confidence.

Another benefit from the previous exercise is that it can throw out some of the rules or beliefs you are running. Beliefs determine your expectations for yourself, others, your horses, in fact every aspect of your life. For Stephen, these included the opinion that eventing is the ultimate test, that competing in all three sections well is a professional standard, that people will respect you if you perform well, that you can keep improving.

Beliefs can often be spotted from the rules you make up and throw into your everyday language. Statements such as 'sitting trot is difficult', 'you need a warmblood to win at dressage these days', or 'only people with sponsors can afford to compete at national level' are examples. Almost everything we say will link back to an opinion and belief. They operate at every level, from simple rules to deeply held philosophies.

They are created by 'reference experiences': the things you have seen, heard, read and experienced that determine what you now think about any topic. Beliefs may come from school, parents or a strong influence in our lives such as a grandparent. They are often supportive when we take them on and they act as a crutch, which makes them important to us. Life is easier too; you never need to think or decide what to do, just follow them.

Over time these ideas can become generalized and so quite fixed and

Once you understand what is motivating
you, it is easy to recognize why little
incidents can affect your confidence

unchanging because we tend to think that what we believe will always be true: one day you may recognize they are holding you back, or that you are applying them in more and more areas of your life where they are not appropriate. Or perhaps you will just live with them, although life with out-of-date beliefs can become difficult in a fast changing world. A moment's thought will allow you to see that, in fact, many beliefs have changed throughout your life where they're not appropriate any more.

Belief changing and reconciling conflicts in values and identity is the area in which NLP excels. However, making these changes is highly personal and needs to be done by working with an experienced practitioner you trust on your specific situation. It is therefore not discussed further in this section, although there is plenty of information available if you want to pursue this. (*See* Further Reading on page 188.)

When you change a belief you will also change a lot of behaviour. However, when you try to change your behaviour it is unlikely to stick if it conflicts with a strongly held belief. Core beliefs about who you are are often at the heart of your personality and have the greatest impact on your behaviour and experience. They are often laid down very early in life. Useful beliefs give an empowering permission and motivation to use your skills to the full.

So whenever you notice one of your beliefs the question to ask is, 'Is it useful and how does it serve me?' Notice which beliefs you are engaged in that work for you, which ones it would be useful to let go of, and which ones would be useful to have.

To summarize, values and beliefs drive your behaviour and so determine your actual capability and performance. Because of this, beliefs have a powerful self-fulfilling effect. As Henry Ford once said: 'Whether you believe you can or you can't, you're right!'

Knowing what you want

Have you ever noticed how the good riders always seem to be able to stay positive and brush off setbacks, while for the more negative riders things often seem to go from bad to worse, and they continually bemoan their lack of luck and blame other people or their horses?

Of course, it does seem as if all their bad luck and lack of success justifies their misery, but did you realize that this attitude can actually cause it? This process of thinking is called the 'success circle' and is an example of what is sometimes referred to as self-fulfilling prophecy. Because it is a cycle of thinking, the self-fulfilling prophecy can be tackled at different points: expectation, changing behaviours or noticing improvements.

At a simple level, if you believe you are a 'good' rider, comparative to your experience, you will be aware of all the best bits of your riding and handling horses, and your confidence will be boosted. On the other hand, if you believe you are a 'bad' or 'nervous' rider, you will magnify all the little mistakes you make out of all proportion. This will then justify a series of negative thoughts about yourself that will actually affect your riding, simply because you are focusing on what is going wrong.

The first key to resolve this is in putting statements into the positive. For example, 'I don't want to feel scared when I go out hacking' is not a positive thought. It focuses attention on what you don't want, on feeling scared. And by putting the thought of feeling scared into your thinking, it becomes a part of your response. Instead you should develop the habit of saying what you do want; for example, 'I want to feel confident and calm when I go out hacking'.

So often we only know and talk about what we don't want, and that is just like going to the supermarket with a list of everything you don't need that day. It would be thousands of things! Imagine shopping like that, having to check every item on every shelf! Apart from being inefficient, it becomes an overwhelming task as there are limitless lists of what we don't want. Do you do this when you

> So often we only know and talk
> about what we don't want.

think about what you desire from your life? This is one of the reasons why 'positive thinking' can be so effective – it is a more focused approach.

Even better, a positive thought will lead to positive planning, more proactive actions and therefore, positive behaviours and performance. Conversely, where you choose to think negatively, it can lead to negative consequences. Each way of thinking will self-perpetuate, so the challenge is to be able to catch the negatives and turn them into more constructive ways of looking at the situation.

Steps to a positive approach

- O Start with a positive belief and image of yourself.

- O Holding this in mind, however simple, will help you build a more positive attitude about yourself.

- O This way of thinking then leads to more positive expectations about how you will behave and perform.

- O This expectation means that you will start noticing when you behave differently and more positively, and so you start to notice the little improvements in performance.

- O As you start to notice these improvements, positive beliefs will grow.

Joanne's story   When Joanne explored this approach, she discovered that her thinking and behaviour ran as follows. She would say to herself, 'Ever since the accident, I'm scared of going hacking so perhaps I shouldn't go today.' She would then go into lots of displacement activity, taking her time over mucking out, tacking up, having an extra cup of coffee and putting off going out while all the time running scenarios in her head that built up the feeling of tension. She would often end up in tears and not go out at all. When she did get on her horse, the hack would often be very short or they would turn around and come home at the slightest reaction or untoward event.

Joanne knew that the slightest thing like a slight spook or a bird flying up nearby could become a reason to return home, and on dustbin day she would not even consider riding out. This is the behaviour of filtering for everything that could or was going wrong. By doing this she was feeding the memory of her accident and creating new, imagined events that were even worse than the original.

Not surprisingly, since the body responds to the imagination, Joanne began to get the feelings of nervousness, butterflies in her stomach, temperature change, and these too often escalated into panic attacks. Even on the good days, she would ride in a tense way, with short reins, gripping with her knees and leaning forward.

Joanne's breakthrough, put in terms of the success cycle, happened when she recognized the effect her position was having on her horse. First she saw herself on video, then she looked at other riders on video coping with spooky moments. In a series of lessons in the school she then worked on her position and realized that rather than leaning forward in a tense way, she was actually safer sitting up and being able to lean back if the horse were to jump forward. With a taller upper body, she was able to relax her legs more. This also had the effect of helping her look around and be more aware of her surroundings so that she could notice where the horse's attention was focused.

When she did this she saw that, at first, she was looking for what would cause the horse to spook or would make her feel scared. From her new 'safer' sitting-up position, she set herself the task of noticing her response and choosing how to behave. We deliberately worked on riding in 'spooky' areas of the

hold the thought

Positive thinking leads to better performance, which in turn, builds up robust beliefs and influences behaviour.

school and put little tests in place, like a coat or rug on the fence and poles and cones on the ground to ride over and through. Joanne learned that even if the horse began to tense or become distracted, she could relax it by increasing her effectiveness focusing on her position.

This new position also helped her to become aware of her breathing. She actually had a little mantra, 'breathe in the beautiful day ...', which she would say to herself as she looked out between her horse's ears. Steadily her position and relaxation improved as did her awareness, and her unconscious was able to move off 'full alert' as she noticed more and rode with more attention on her surroundings and the horse's reaction.

For Joanne, the belief of 'I enjoy hacking out' could only really build up once she'd had some of these positive experiences and put herself more in control of her posture, breathing and behaviour. However, when that belief was supported by some good experiences, she was able to adjust it to 'I enjoy hacking out safely'. By doing this, she acknowledged her unconscious mind's need for reassurance and this had the affect of kicking-in a new awareness of her responsibility to herself to be prepared.

She decided simply not to hack out on the routes that had faster traffic and a bad bend, bought a better high-visibility vest to wear, always took her mobile phone with her and always told someone what route she was taking. She adjusted her riding times so that she could hack with a friend at least once a week. With all these changes in place the belief then became stronger and stronger. A year later she did her first sponsored ride and was thinking of learning more about endurance riding.

Joanne's story clearly illustrates how positive thinking actually leads to better performance, how good performance will in turn help to build up more robust beliefs, and how those beliefs will influence behaviour, which then means you can think more positively … and so the cycle continues.

Linda Kohanov, in *The Tao of Equus*, describes this approach well when she relates to the need to remain calm while handling a potentially challenging situation. She refers to the alert yet meditative approach used in martial arts as follows: ' … Take deep breaths, keep your body fully in the present and your mind in the recent future. Don't let the past get in your way …'

The importance of positive focus

Useful beliefs normally act as empowering permissions to use your skills to the full, while negative ones act as limitations.

When you catch yourself making more negative statements, consider the standard of comparison you are making. In other words, who or what are you comparing yourself with? For instance, if you catch yourself saying, 'Oh, I'm no good at jumping', ask yourself 'no good at jumping *compared to who?*' If you are comparing yourself to your instructor or to a professional competitor, is it surprising you're not as good when you haven't ridden as much, or as many horses, or jumped as many fences?

When you compare yourself or make such generalizations, check out the basis for the comparison; accepting how unrealistic it is to be as good as someone with more experience is a quick way to boost your confidence. Even if you are comparing yourself against other riders of a closer standard, take into account aspects such as how much time you have available to ride, how much experience you have, your horse's age and history.

Now think about what you need to do to build a bit more skill into your riding; decide on a couple of action points that will make it happen. This could be as simple as looking at photos or videos of yourself riding and photos of a rider you admire, choosing just two things to do differently in

> Accepting how unrealistic it is to be as good as someone with more experience is a quick way to boost your confidence.

terms of your position so as to make the pictures look more similar. Do your hands need to be in a different place, are your legs wrapped around the horse in the same way? Your instructor or a friend can help if you can't see where or how you need to develop your position.

case study

Stephen's story

Stephen's story is a good example of how comparison can really undermine your confidence. As a young professional rider Stephen knew it was important to take his teaching and stable management exams so that he could gain appropriate insurance and build his reputation. He also wanted to compete and had a young horse of his own in addition to a couple he was schooling and competing for other people.

All went fine at home but in a series of shows he suddenly 'lost his nerve' when going into the ring. He tensed up, went wrong in the test or forgot the jumping course. A couple of errors escalated into a pattern of some little mistake every time out, even if it was just forgetting some piece of equipment. It soon became a bit of a joke and he was teased a lot, but he also sensed the irritation that the owners felt when his silly mistakes wasted their entry fees. Then he realized he was finding an excuse not to compete.

Just as Joanne had discovered, his focus had become what he was getting wrong rather than what he was doing right. But his situation went deeper than that. When he eventually came for a private one-to-one session, it finally dawned on him that he had deep-seated fears about not being good enough and what other people would think of him. At a deep unconscious level, these little mistakes were 'proving' to him that he did not have what it took to be a professional.

As the explanation about Stephen's values earlier illustrated, being respected as a professional was an important value and identity for him. No wonder he was starting to feel threatened; his run of repeated mistakes meant people were starting to show a lessening respect for him.

Equally, he realized that he had been letting the same mistakes repeat themselves, which indicated to him that he had not been improving' and which also did not support him in his desired self-image of being a professional! As soon as he perceived this, he was able to make some simple changes to how he learned dressage tests and jumping courses. After all, as a youngster, learning dressage tests had been a chore his mum had nagged him about and which he hadn't taken that seriously!

Now that he understood the wider significance of course walking and planning how to ride a test well by knowing it inside out, his attitude to the 'chore' changed. In some ways, this represented quite a subtle shift in his thinking but it indicates how a potential problem can start, and indeed how easy it is to take action once you realize why something is getting to you.

Linking beliefs with behaviours

The 'logical level' is a means of understanding the relationship between what matters to you and how you actually behave and so finding where the real root of an issue or approach lies. It was developed by Robert Dilts, one of the leading thinkers in NLP.

The concept is usually represented as a pyramid, where each level impacts on the one below it so that all are interrelated. The highest level at the top is your 'mission' or purpose, then identity, and below it are beliefs and values. These in turn drive the skills and capabilities we demonstrate. These link to behaviours, what you actually do, and at the bottom are the environmental factors such as where you are and what you are wearing.

It helps to plot the relationship or hierarchy that links our everyday environmental choices and behaviour together with who we are and

hold the thought

> It is easy to take action
> once you realize why something is
> getting to you.

what we believe. When these are aligned, there is an unmistakable state of inner harmony and improved performance.

In Stephen's case study, he realized that being a professional (identity) meant that he set certain values on being respected and on his continuing improvement. By learning how to remember tests and courses in order to ride them effectively (belief and capability), he could satisfy these values. He therefore spent more time on preparing and learning the tests and courses (behaviour), and made sure he always checked out the arena for things that might affect how he rode in them (environment).

A dressage rider who I work with found that her purpose in riding dressage was 'to create art with nature'. This sounds quite far removed from actually riding. However, when you really understand what matters to you and what motivates you, it will often take you to this sort of description. Knowing that this was her definition, the rider redefined herself as, ' I am a classical dressage rider', an identity level statement. Only one word, but to her it meant the difference between competitive, pressured riding and the joy of riding with lightness and elegance, training the horse to be a partner with her. Competitions were simply a means of showing others this partnership.

The beliefs that accompany being a classical dressage rider were many and varied. In particular, she believed she had a responsibility to ride well in order that the horse could carry her easily. She also had a set of beliefs around the horse's mental state and its need to be allowed to be a horse. Providing more turn-out time, and letting her horses relate to each other were an area she had to change in order to behave in line with these beliefs.

The capabilities she had as a classical dressage rider included staying relaxed and calm. It is a deeper level of control – more about her self-control and ability to stay relaxed and so help the horse be softer.

Christina's story As a young adult, Christina had enjoyed the thrill of eventing to affiliated intermediate level. She lived in 'the fast lane' with a successful, well-paid career. She was very positive, especially as success seemed to come so easily. Some of her core beliefs were to do with taking on challenges, seeking out opportunities, making things happen and enjoying life's experiences to the full. It was, therefore, not surprising that her loss of confidence when she returned to riding was wrapped up in these beliefs and the identity they stemmed from.

We spent more time in a coaching mode, discussing her motivation and what mattered to her rather than doing the ridden exercises I used with Joanne. In fortnightly sessions we explored her beliefs and her dreams about the future. It was a significant revelation to her that her newfound role as a mother meant she was now, in many ways, a different person. With the responsibility of children came a new identity and with it, a need to curb her happy-go-lucky approach to riding and life. Always at the back of her mind would be the responsibility of looking after the children, and thus the need to look after herself more. She needed to think more in the long term.

By exploring her identity as a mother, and the sort of relationship with her children that she wanted, Christina was able to identify ways in which riding could become a key part of their family life. She wanted her children to have confidence around animals and an awareness of, and respect for, nature; something that horses in the family could provide so well. She also wanted to be an example to them of making the most of life.

Knowing how much the world was changing, she wanted her children to be bold and confident enough to try out new ideas and be aware of the need to keep learning. Rather than letting her new role as a mother limit her, she decided she would now be proactive and seek out opportunities in order to be an example to her children. Yet it was important to honour the responsibility to look after herself so she could look after them.

In effect, she 'reframed' her beliefs around making things happen and enjoying life to include the responsibility of children. She decided to focus on dressage and show jumping instead of eventing, and therefore decided to buy a laid-back warmblood that would be easier for the children to relate to.

hold the thought

> Knowing what is important to you about horses and riding helps you to be confident with them.

My conversations with her appear quite simplistic when quickly summarized like this. The most important point to grasp as you read about Christina is the sincerity with which she worked through the beliefs and capabilities she needed to live up to in her 'new' identity as a mother, and the depth of self-understanding it gave her.

As both Stephen and Christina's examples show, by understanding what your purpose and core values are, you can quickly refer to them in order to make compatible decisions. It can have significant impacts on your behaviour: think about the men and women who take a stand for what they really believe in. Such people have consistent themes that guide their actions and their values. These motivate them and all their actions are aligned towards achieving them.

case study

Joanne's story Joanne mapped her original behaviours against the logical levels: how she was and how she wanted to be. This helped her understand where she had to make the most adjustments. First she put in place some environmental safety nets: a high-visibility jacket, riding with other people and choosing her routes more carefully. In terms of her behaviour, she resolved to act as if she were a relaxed rider, focusing on her breathing, saying her mantra, and really sitting up and looking around her. At a capability level, she identified that she needed to handle her horse more confidently and calmly – she had to admit that she was often too shrill and flappy around him, thus putting him on edge!

Joanne recognized that she already had some strong positive beliefs about horses, and now simply added to those the belief that she was responsible for their shared experiences. Through our work together she was able to change her identity statement from, 'I am a nervous rider' to 'I am a responsible rider'. Some time later she happily rang me to announce, 'I am an endurance rider!'

The power of visualization

The popular understanding of NLP sports psychology is more about effective visualization and changing self-talk than beliefs and values. After all, these are much simpler concepts than the effect of identity upon behaviour. Yet how we visualize a memory or future experience will impact it just as much. Below I outline how these two areas work together to support change work at belief and value level as already discussed.

NLP offers an understanding of how your brain sorts and stores the information it is bombarded with. Think about it – everything you have ever experienced was absorbed through your senses: sight, hearing, touch, smell and taste. At any moment there are millions of pieces of information you can take in through these five senses, most of which your unconscious mind will filter out as they are completely irrelevant to what you are doing and thinking.

This leaves the conscious mind free to talk, plan and generally be rational, so you will only be aware of about seven things at any given moment. The unconscious mind also streamlines certain tasks, after enough repetition, so that we do not need to consciously think about what to do. This makes it very efficient at carrying out habitual tasks. Consider how easily you can now tie up a haynet or put together a bridle compared to the very first time you tried! This helps to explain how being able to trust the unconscious or intuitive mind to respond appropriately is another skill to develop; the good riders can 'just do it' because the conscious mind does not get in the way!

One of the key contributions that NLP offers to the field of psychology is an understanding of how the mind has stored the detail of each sense for each memory. By bringing out these details, it is possible to re-experience a 'good' memory and make it even better, and more significantly, to change a

hold the thought

It is possible to re-experience a 'good' memory and make it even better, and to change a 'bad' memory.

'bad' memory. It is then surprisingly easy to put yourself in control of your thoughts and the emotional responses they generate.

Often our best experiences are stored as large, moving colour pictures, with pleasing sounds and feelings associated with them. A negative experience is therefore best stored as a small, black and white, still image, like an old photo, with low sounds and no emotions or feelings attached to it.

However, when we get it around the wrong way and remember our bad experiences as huge, full-colour movies, with all the sounds and drama, creating scary or stressful feelings, it's not surprising that we start feeling stressed at the thought of them. It also explains why a bad experience can change your ability to do something, even though the rational part of you understands it was a past event.

This process works because memory and imagination share the same circuitry, the same brain and the nerve endings through your body so that one can affect the other. This is why visualization, self-talk and the importance of correct practice are important to put learnings 'into the muscle'. This term refers to the need for the body to have a repeated physical experience in order to improve your ability. When you need to change an established pattern of 'bad' behaviour, you will need more teaching than if you were learning the right behaviour from new.

Returning to Christina's case study, we can see how such simple changes can be very powerful in enhancing a memory.

Christina's story Christina had a great memory of competing at a novice event when she and her horse had completed each section almost foot perfect. In her memory she had a picture, in colour, of horse and rider from the side, caught in mid-air over a jump. It was a fairly small picture and about fifteen feet away. There was no sound and no particular feelings. When I asked her whether or not she was smiling in her picture, Christina actually leant forward to have a look – remember, it was just in her mind!

I suggested that she imagine it was closer, about three feet away. This simple suggestion made the memory come alive for he and she began to describe the event, who else she had met there, who the judge was, some comments on the score sheet, and what the going was like. She couldn't believe the details she was remembering! As she reviewed the experience, we realized that what had once been a small, still picture was now a movie. I wondered if she could make it larger, right up to life size. Her face lit up as she took it all in; now she was imagining it as if it was really happening, so that she could see the horse's ears, the course she was riding and feel each stride and jump. She could hear the sounds of the horse, his thundering hooves and breathing, and her friends cheering as she jumped the fences and came through the finish.

By bringing the event to life again with those few simple questions, Christina was able to appreciate how much she had enjoyed jumping and became determined to jump again. And she is loving it!

Effective visualization is about positive mental images, whether these are memories, fantasies or a combination of both. It is an activity within the nervous system and so can directly influence the body in several ways. Certain types of visualization can even stimulate immune-system functioning and other healing processes. In setting outcomes or goals, having an image of what you see, hear and feel helps the unconscious mind to set up the appropriate behaviours.

Because imagination involves recombining the elements of previous experiences, it can be used to create dreams, visualize outcomes and imagine the longer-term impact of these dreams. It is one of the core tools in NLP, used directly in several of the change techniques. The outcome process is one

> Effective visualization is about
> forming positive mental images,
> whether these are memories, fantasies
> or a combination of both.

of these. When you imagine a dream in your mind's eye and the result is pleasing to you, you can recognize and mobilize the resources that are needed to turn that dream into a reality.

Christina's example illustrates how NLP can be used to remember a good memory and even make it feel better than it was. You can take an ability or resource that you have in another area of your life, such as confidence at work, and add it into your riding. These resources may be happy memories of behaviours, skills or capabilities, or involve reminding yourself about empowering beliefs and your strongest sense of identity or spirituality.

It is important to break the cycle of negative thinking by changing states, for once you have changed your emotional state, say from nervousness to calmness, the horse can follow. NLP provides a clever technique called 'Anchoring' which facilitates this, allowing you to recall useful emotional states, such as confidence or serenity, whenever you need them by giving yourself a signal. We all have many anchors set up already – after all, when you hear your name said in a certain tone or see a photo of a special memory it will bring up a response.

This Anchoring technique is often used to take the nervous rider to a better emotional state from which he or she can act more resourcefully. I used it with Stephen, Christina and Joanne to give them a simple trigger they could activate for themselves whenever they needed it.

Unconscious intent

One of the joys of using the NLP sports psychology approach is that it enables your 'unconscious intent' to get to work so that you can stop trying so hard. It's like pushing to open a door when, by looking at it, you notice that it opens towards you. Have you ever said, 'I wish I could ride like that', 'I want to keep my horses at home', 'I'd love a new saddle', or something similar, and then looked back some time later and realized it had come true?

If so, what did you do to make it happen? Maybe nothing 'consciously', because just by focusing your unconscious attention on what you wanted, you began the process of making it happen. This is due to a part of your brain called the Reticular Activating System (RAS). It is responsible for screening out all information except what will be helpful to you. It acts like a magnet, attracting the information and opportunities that can help you achieve your goal more quickly.

Starting to actively switch on your ability to achieve what you really want simply by thinking about it sounds dreamlike, but it has been scientifically proven through studying the mind-body interaction. Think about what it is like waiting for your turn to go into the ring at a competition. As you wait, you may notice yourself thinking about the performance you are about to give. You may become more confident, or less, more agitated or indeed calmer. Compare this with the feeling of waiting for someone you are riding out with as they mount, where there is no competitive pressure. Most people feel very different. Your response to a new event is determined by your previous memories of similar contexts, which will dictate how you behave.

This study of the cause and effect in a context is called cybernetics, and it can be considered the cornerstone of NLP. It explains how to run your mind more actively or constructively, although there is only scope to mention it briefly here.

Basically, once you know what you really want, your unconscious mind starts to adapt and adjust your behaviour to move closer to your goals. This is

> Your response to a new event is determined by your previous memories, which will dictate how you behave.

because the brain is a 'cybernetic mechanism' and once you are clear about your outcome, your brain will start to organize all your unconscious behaviour in order to attain it. In NLP this is called unconscious intent, and being able to utilize it is a simple process. It is where the 'softer' world of affirmations and visualization come into play.

An affirmation is much more than an unbelievable statement that you repeat endlessly to yourself. To say, 'I am a calm and confident rider' will not be convincing until you really believe it. While you are working on changing your beliefs it is much better to ask yourself a proactive question such as, 'What can I do today that will help me feel calmer when I ride?' or 'What can I do to understand the horse better now?' This will give you ideas of what you can proactively work on and will help your emotional state.

One of the first approaches to building an effective affirmation is to understand the positive intention behind your fear – what could the benefit be? Although it sounds a bit unreal, imagine that having a confidence crisis when approaching a jump in fact has a deep benefit. It could be that the unconscious mind is telling you that you are about to do something for which you are not yet ready or are unprepared. By preventing you from taking the jump, it could be protecting your safety!

When faced with a situation that the unconscious thinks will be potentially dangerous, the mind will seek to provide security by sending alerts to the conscious mind. These tend to increase in intensity, starting with a little voice saying 'be careful' to almost preventing the rider from actually riding, with stomach upsets and panic attacks.

So when your unconscious mind is *that* concerned for your safety, perhaps it is worth having a really careful review of what you are doing. Frustrating though it is, a pause in your progress now, while you go back to consolidate some basic skills, could pay dividends later when your confidence means you can easily hack, jump, or whatever it is you want to do in the future.

As an example of this, Joanne discovered that the reason she was beginning to have panic attacks while out hacking was because her unconscious mind knew she tended to be a bit dreamy and slow to react, so it put her on a super-full alert that went too far. By changing her routes, going out with another person and being more aware when she rode, she was able to reduce her attacks considerably. She finally moved yards so that she could be off the roads and on a better network of bridleways instead.

Sometimes, really focusing on your position and breathing puts you into more conscious control, and you can experiment with acting as if you were confident, calm, or whatever your particular solution is. This new reference experience allows your unconscious and conscious mind to believe that you can ride in a different way. Your instructor could assist you to do this and you could have a video or series of photos of you riding to help you really analyze your position and effectiveness.

In my work with riders who need to build their confidence and overcome fears, the way I find most effective for the majority of cases is to be aware of small incremental improvements, so that the comfort zone grows daily or weekly. Starting small makes it manageable, and becoming aware of a feedback loop rapidly builds momentum. Some clients want and can cope with dramatic changes in thinking, but most need time, feedback and willpower.

One easy way to give yourself that feedback is to keep a daily notebook for your riding progress. At the front, write down what you would really like your riding to aspire to, keeping it in the positive as explained earlier. You may choose to add in some goals and there are details about how to set these later in the section.

Each day for at least three months, take just five to ten minutes of quiet time to reflect on your riding. This could be in the car just after you have ridden, or perhaps in the evening.

> Be aware of small improvements, so
> that your comfort zone grows daily.

Keeping your notebook

○ Set yourself a mini step of one little thing
that will be improved or different next time
you ride or are around horses and note it.

○ Even if you are not with horses everyday, you
can have little steps such as watching an
instructional video, reading a chapter of a
book, browsing the web on a revelant topic,
or simply thinking about what you want to do.
The next day just put a tick or cross
according to whether you did that step or not.

○ Write down something you noticed that day
related to your riding goals. It could be how
other people coped in a similar situation,
how you reacted to something, or a quote or
saying that struck you.

○ Add what you learned from that experience. If
you did not like it, write down what you
would have preferred to have seen, heard or
felt.

When you look back through this diary after a period of time you will be
able to track how much you have developed through actively thinking about
your riding in this way. The simple daily notebook is an easy tool to utilize,
and it helps to keep you aware of your performance. However, you will really
add power to your journey towards more confident riding if you take the
time to set some clear goals against which to measure your progress.

The importance of setting goals

Why is there so much emphasis in sports psychology on goal setting and knowing what you want? Put simply, your mind will generate actions based on your existing habits and reactions or motivating plans. Where your existing reactions are letting you down, you need to be strongly motivated to change them. Otherwise you will continue to do just what you have done before.

Writing down your goals and sub goals is an excellent means of focusing your mind on what you want. So often people set goals that others think they should have, or in order to keep up with their friends. However, when something is not right for you and your circumstances, it will not motivate you and may become a source of worry.

Remember that no goal achievement or learning is ever an upward-only curve: there are setbacks and delays, so it is useful to consider what you have learned and what you will do differently next time. It is always acceptable to adjust the plan in the light of these learnings. What matters is that you continue to develop and learn through the goals you have set with your horse. Keep goals that are really important to you on display and share them with friends. This will serve as a constant reminder to you about your plans. Discussing the ups and downs on the way with your friends will help to encourage you to keep going towards your destination.

It is important to keep track of your goals and your progress towards them as this will motivate you to keep going. Tick each action step as you do it and mark off when you achieve the different milestones. You could also build in little rewards to yourself when you pass them. You can simply keep smaller goals in your notebook. By looking back every month or so, you will find you have accomplished things you had forgotten about.

It is best to start with the 'big picture', a long enough time scale, maybe two to three years, as you are then giving your unconscious mind a clear direction to follow. Joanne's story summarizes the goal-setting process.

What matters is that you continue to develop and learn through the goals you have set with your horse.

case study

Joanne's story At first it took some persuasion to get Joanne to state a two- to three-year goal. The thought of committing herself to being able to do something she could not currently face was daunting. I reminded her that the goal could be moved further into the future if necessary, the key point was to give her unconscious something to hook on to. She decided her dream was to be able to enjoy a ten-mile sponsored ride and complete a Le Trec competition.

With this as a start point she had to imagine a halfway ambition, and she set the shorter-term goal of hacking out confidently with other people within a year. Working back from that, she decided on a six-month goal and cantering around a field in a lesson was agreed. Before she could do that, she wanted to feel more confident coping with spooks and cantering in the school, two goals to work towards over the following three to four months.

In order to achieve these first two milestones, she set herself some action steps including watching her instructor and other riders coping with spooky and lively horses, and really improving her position and depth of seat. Rather than just completing tasks, there are usually skills and capabilities you need to develop in order to achieve the goal. This is usually where effective goal setting starts: are you able to identify how you need to develop and improve?

Joanne also had some lunge lessons and made time to watch advanced riders working young horses. Videos proved to her that her position really was better when she sat up as instructed, and steadily she got used to that way of riding. She became so focused on everything she had to do that she ended up forgetting to feel nervous and, needless to say, she was thrilled when she completed her first sponsored ride within a year.

Joanne's story highlights the methodical nature of effective goal setting; identifying a number of small steps that add up to help you make big changes. Keeping a record of what you do, and how you cope with any setbacks, is an important part of making progress as you become more aware of the little changes you are implementing.

As I have already said, progress is not an upward-only curve. It is important to recognize that there will be some setbacks and what matters is how you cope with them. Episodes that may have previously set you back, like a tractor suddenly appearing and the horse spooking, mean that you may need to measure your progress in terms of remaining calm and keeping the horse's attention on you instead. One day you will look back and see that it all adds up to an unmistakable improvement.

Set up a session with your trainer to take stock of your riding, looking at where you have progressed from, where you want to get to, and how you are going to do it. Make sure you think about the amount of time and money you are prepared to put towards achieving your goal and how you will keep track.

Being able to look at your situation from a number of different perspectives is another easy way to make progress and build your confidence as it will enable you to gain all sorts of new insights. Too often we stay in the 'me' space, seeing things just from our own point of view: our feelings and emotions, our reasoning behind our choice of action, in short, what makes us tick. Most people are good at this, but if you only think about things from the 'me' perspective, you can lack empathy with other people and your horse.

It is useful to remember that the horse is always in first position, thinking about what he needs for an easier life, being simply motivated by safety, food or social acceptance. He has not set a goal of going clear nor does he know the subtleties of competition scoring. As section 2: *Understanding the Horse* highlights the horse is a highly perceptive animal and it is valuable to remember that he is also a prey animal. By understanding your horse better, you will be able to respond more calmly and appropriately to any given situation concerning him.

When you put yourself into the body and mindset of your horse, it is like stepping into his shoes. It is the perfect place from where to gain a better understanding of his perspective and you can get a sense of what it is like to actually be a horse, to feel, see, hear and even smell and taste as he does.

By understanding your horse better, you will be able to respond more appropriately to any given situation.

case study

Joanne's story Joanne certainly had a shock when she understood what a burden she was placing on her horse by being so nervous. She could relate it to a time at work when her boss was under immense stress, and how everyone else picked it up and began to behave either in similar ways or had time off ill. Work was not an enjoyable place to be and Joanne had in fact left her job because of it. When she imagined what it would be like to be her horse, she actually became quite upset as she realized how much he could be affected by her tension.

She resolved to behave like a team leader, to set the schooling and hacking environment up so that her needs for feeling secure were being met; these were the safety nets discussed earlier. She resolved to act 'as if' more, focusing on her breathing, reciting her mantra and really sitting up and looking around her. These are examples of how behaviour and environment can be adjusted. Joanne already had strong beliefs and, through our work together, was changing her identity statement from, 'I am a nervous rider' to 'I handle my horse confidently and calmly'.

Another perspective to take is the observer position. Here, one stands back and takes a completely rational, uninvolved view of the situation, detached from all the emotions involved. Imagine you are a wise old owl watching the incident going on without being drawn into the emotions and actual event. This is a position an instructor or judge can take, able to ask, 'What does this person need in order to handle the situation better and progress?'

Also consider whether the horse you ride is right for you. Riders looking back at problem situations often see they were trying to prove something to themselves or others. Perhaps they had limited knowledge about what the horse 'should' do or how they 'should' be able to ride it. Frequently, they realize that they were riding or handling a horse beyond their capabilities.

Sometimes people relate to these experiences at a metaphorical level and see that they needed the experience in order to fully understand themselves and be prepared to make changes in their lives. There is an NLP process by which they can let go of a previous accident or incident by understanding what they learned from it and what they would do differently if the same situation started to happen again.

I would always suggest, however, that rather than seek these sorts of challenges, you select a more laid-back horse appropriate to your level of ability. Always be aware of your responsibility as a rider to build your confidence through self-knowledge and steady improvement rather than expect the horse to carry your stresses for you.

Pat Parelli, the US-based natural horsemanship trainer, summarizes the relationship with the horse well. He states: 'Horses are a great metaphor for our own personal development. They hold a mirror to us everyday, reflecting every mental and emotional bobble! ... Horses have no concern for our egos. They tell it like it is, offering us the opportunity to develop the patience of Job, the courage of a lion tamer, the gentleness of a mother with her new-born baby, the timing of a kung fu black belt and the focus of a world leader... The horse, like no other living creature, teaches us to become more than we are because until we are what he needs us to be, he'll give us mediocre results.'

hold the thought

Be aware of your responsibility as a rider to build your confidence through self-knowledge and steady improvement.

The confidence to change

Today few people are 'born in the saddle', so the learning process starts later than it did for those children who were able to ride because the family lived in the country and had horses as a matter of course.

Often, people learning to ride will have lessons just once or twice a week, possibly on a different horse each time. For adults, office-based work and commuting limits the opportunity for daily contact with horses. Because horses are less and less a part of everyday life, experiences and fears from other parts of our lives can limit our ability to act with confidence when riding. So, just because someone impresses you with their boldness and bravado, riding difficult horses, jumping and galloping, it does not mean that they are the right teacher for you. Indeed, the contrast in approaches could actually reinforce that feeling of inadequacy. It is about finding the depth of knowledge and an instructor's ability to know what you need for your progress. Any instructor who makes you feel inadequate is to be avoided, and a true coaching style is helpful since the best way of helping riders who lack confidence is to assist them access to their own resources.

At the same time you need to make a commitment to yourself, and the instructor, to make changes. Most good instructors teach because they love the thrill of accompanying someone on their journey of discovery and celebrating each little success from week to week. Each step the pupil acknowledges and delights in is like the equivalent progress for the teacher.

Looking back, after having developed their confidence and accomplishing the things that mattered to them in their riding, most people are intrigued to realize how their 'fearful' behaviour was actually protecting them – it had just gone too far. Remember Joanne's discovery that the reason she was beginning to have panic attacks while she was out hacking was because her unconscious mind knew that she could become too casual. Once Christina

○ Put aside enough to pay for the right instructor, even if it means you have lessons less often.

○ Spend time researching and selecting the right one for you. Try to watch them teaching before committing yourself. Your confidence should be above only considering the price.

○ When watching them teach, imagine you are the rider on the horse and notice how their style of instruction would work for you.

○ Remember, just because your friend is motivated by a particular instructor doesn't necessarily mean you will be because you are both motivated differently.

○ Check that the instructor's qualifications and experience suit your needs. Accidents can happen and a professional instructor will have a first-aid qualification and professional liability insurance, usually through a national registration scheme.

○ Take time to set your goals, track your progress and acknowledge small steps along the way.

○ Once you have chosen an instructor, you need to work openly enough to allow his or her approach to take effect. Such two-way commitment allows a longer-term view of the training you need, rather than a quick fix. It allows your instructor to be honest with you.

had recognized the impact of her new identity as a mother, she was able to focus on the example she wanted to be to her children, a blend of boldness and considered thinking. And once Stephen had let go of the early incidents and beliefs about being watched and the need to always be the best, he was able to be himself and make considerable progress.

It is interesting to discover that when you change, other people will be affected. There is likely to be an unconscious, subtle pressure on you to stay just as you were because, otherwise, your friends and family have to change too.

Suppose you previously wore the equivalent of a big badge saying, 'I'm scared of hacking/jumping/competing'. Now imagine yourself walking into the yard without it, and acting with confidence, with calmness, and with determination. What would your instructor say instead? How would the other people in the yard respond to you? Chances are that, at one level, they preferred you as you were because now, their understanding of you and your relationship with them may have to adjust. This is why, with major changes, it is sometimes easier to make a clean break in order to be able to behave differently.

Very few dreams can be achieved by continuing to do what you have always done. So respect the horse as your teacher and think about the lessons you learn together. Make the commitment to change your attitudes and beliefs, and so enjoy riding with more confidence than ever before. You can do it!

hold the thought

Be bold, take the journey the horse is inviting you on and enjoy what it has to offer!

Further Reading

Greenberger, Dennis and Padesky, Christine *Mind Over Mood*
    (The Guilford Press, New York) 1995

Havens, Ronald and Walters, Catherine *Hypnotherapy Scripts*
    (Brunner/Mazel Publications, New York) 1989

Howard, Judy *The Bach Flower Remedies Step by Step* (CW Daniel) 1990

Jeffers, Susan *Feel the Fear and Do It Anyway* (Arrow) 1991

Kohanov, Linda *The Tao of Equus* (New World Library) 2001

Looker, Terry and Gregson, Olga *Managing Stress*
    (Hodder and Stoughton) 1997

Midkiff, Mary D. *She Flies Without Wings*
    (Dell Publishing, Random House Inc) 2001

Morrison, Liz *Simple Steps to Riding Success* (David and Charles) 2002

Rashid, Mark *Horses Never Lie* (David and Charles) 2004

Seymour, J. and O'Connor, J. *Introducing NLP* (Thorsons) 1993

Thompson, Alf *Handbook for Students* (Salford College, England) 2001

Waxman, David *Hartlands Medical and Dental Hypnosis*
    (Bailliere Tindall, London) 1981

For further information of the *Confident Rider Series* of self-hypnosis CDs by Sharon Shinwell see www.confidentrider.co.uk

Titles in the series include:

Jumping with Confidence

Hacking with Confidence

Roadwork with Confidence

For further information on Intelligent Horsemanship see www.intelligenthorsemanship.co.uk

Index